D1172880

Lay My Burden Down

Alvin F. Poussaint, M.D.
Amy Alexander

Lay My Burden Down

Unraveling Suicide and the Mental Health
Crisis among African-Americans

Beacon Press
Boston

Beacon Press
25 Beacon Street
Boston, Massachusetts 02108-2892
www.beacon.org

Beacon Press books
are published under the auspices of
the Unitarian Universalist Association of Congregations.

© 2000 by Alvin F. Poussaint, M.D., and Amy Alexander
All rights reserved
Printed in the United States of America

05 04 03 02 01 00   8 7 6 5 4 3 2 1

Traditional hymn, harmonies by J. Jefferson Cleveland, 1937, and Nerolga Nix,
1933, *Songs of Zion*, copyright 1981 Abingdon Publishers, Nashville.

This book is printed on acid-free paper that meets the uncoated
paper ANSI/NISO specifications for permanence as revised in 1992.

Text design by Wesley B. Tanner/Passim Editions
Composition by Wilsted & Taylor Publishing Services

Library of Congress Cataloging-in-Publication Data
Poussaint, Alvin F.
    Lay my burden down : unraveling suicide and the mental health crisis
among African-Americans / Alvin F. Poussaint and Amy Alexander.
        p.   cm.
    Includes bibliographical references and index.
    ISBN 0-8070-0960-1 (acid-free paper)
    1. Afro-Americans–Suicidal behavior.   2. Afro-Americans–Mental health.
3. Afro-Americans–Social conditions–1975–   I. Alexander, Amy.   II. Title.
E185.625 .P68   2000
616.89'0089'96073–dc21   00-008859

For our brothers,

Kenneth Poussaint and Carl Burton,

and all the members of the

Alexander, Fermon, and Poussaint families

Glory, Glory, Hallelujah

Glory, glory, Hallelujah
Since I laid my burden down.

I feel better, so much better
Since I laid my burden down.

Feel like shouting 'Hallelujah'!
Since I laid my burden down.

I am climbing Jacob's ladder
Since I laid my burden down.

Ev'ry round goes higher and higher
Since I laid my burden down.

Glory, glory, Hallelujah
Since I laid my burden down.

—traditional, *Songs of Zion*

Contents

Prologue

Brothers Remembered

The Star Bethel Missionary Baptist Church is a whitewashed monument to faith on San Pablo Avenue in Oakland, California. It is the tallest building on its block, a three-story fortress surrounded by a tattered shopping district and faded apartment complexes. Its congregation comes from the immediate area, and although members of other ethnic groups have been welcomed, its majority represents a cross section of Oakland's working-class black residents–government workers, day laborers, single mothers, teenagers, children, and retirees.

For several decades Star Bethel has anchored a neighborhood perpetually in transition, an edgy community constantly at the brink of urban decay. Over the years, other stretches of San Pablo Avenue have slid beyond that edge. The black-owned barbershops, restaurants, record stores, and clothing boutiques that once flourished along its several miles have become immigrant-owned enterprises or now turn shuttered faces toward the street. Star Bethel is not the most prosperous of the city's predominantly black Christian churches, but its stucco and wrought-iron bulk has always been a stabilizing presence in this corner of Oakland. In the early-morning hours of February 28, 1979, it provided an unexpected solution for a troubled young black man in distress.

Carl Michael Burton, twenty-five, had lived in Oakland off and on for much of his life. At six feet two inches tall, with a high forehead, wide-set brown eyes, and large, straight white teeth set off by a smooth, caramel-colored complexion, he had been, in better times, a bit of a ladies' man.

As a teenager, Carl had ambitions, and after graduating from Woodrow Wilson High School in San Francisco in 1970 he set out to fulfill them. For almost six years he worked as a union laborer at the Chevron refinery in Richmond. By the mid-1970s he had reached a salary level (about $24,000 a year) that allowed him to buy his mother, Hazel Fermon, a washing machine and dryer for the basement of her home in San Francisco's Ingleside district. Confident and easygoing, Carl was a sharp young man on the go, a child of the civil rights era who believed that hard work would deliver him to the doorstep of personal prosperity. But in 1975, following a visit from a fast-living Midwest-based male cousin who'd "turned him on," Carl had quietly developed an addiction to heroin.

By midwinter of 1979, the clothes that Carl had once maintained with meticulous devotion hung from his large frame in dusty wrinkles. His cousin Michael Carse, an auto mechanic who lived not far from Star Bethel, would often see him marching along the streets of Oakland with a purposeful, militaristic gait, his eyes glazed, his knees snapping upward with each step, his lips moving in a silent cadence. On this particular morning in late February, the mid-length wool coat that Carl wore, its black-and-red checked pattern bristling with grime, did little to keep out the biting Northern California chill, and the crown of thick hair that he had once picked and patted into a splendid full-moon Afro now jutted and peaked in odd angles.

He had spent much of the previous night in a public park not far from Star Bethel, shooting drugs with some other San Pablo Avenue regulars. Before dawn he had turned up at his aunt Sara's apartment building, a low-slung structure on Stanford Street, behind the church. For the next several hours he thrashed and hurled his body against the walls of the small apartment, and his aunt and his cousin Lloyd were unable to calm him or to soothe his moaning cries. Years later, his cousin Michael recalled that Carl's hand and footprints were visible on the interior walls of Sara's apartment: "Whatever he'd been shooting, whatever he was dealing with, it literally had him climbing the walls."

Carl's cousins were aware of his addiction to heroin. They did not know, however, that he'd also taken to shooting methamphetamine, or "speed," into his veins; nor did his cousins know that Carl had been diagnosed with schizophrenia in 1977.

Many times that night Sara begged her nephew to settle down and try to sleep. At daybreak she phoned Carl's mother in San Francisco, only to find her sister gone, already on the way to her job in Richmond. Around 7 A.M., agitated and uncertain, Sara left Stanford Street for work, saying she would phone Hazel again once she reached her office. But by the height of rush hour, Carl was on the street again. This time he walked the twenty yards from his aunt's apartment to an outdoor stairwell on the side of Star Bethel.

He shrugged off his wool coat, folded it, and placed it on the bottom step. Moving stiffly in a white T-shirt and Levi's, he mounted the stairs to the second story of the church, where he came to a locked door.

Reaching out beyond the guardrail, he grabbed the last rung of the fire escape ladder and pulled himself up. He then climbed to the landing on the outside of the third floor, where he was confronted by another locked door. By extending his arms all the way above his head, he could just grip the edge of the roof. Once, twice, perhaps three times his workboots scraped for traction against window hinges as he sought leverage. Finally he managed to hoist himself halfway onto the roof, his stomach and hips pressing into gravel as he swung first one leg, then the other, over the tar-paper rim.

Shortly after 8 A.M., a neighbor spotted Carl pacing along the edge of the church roof overlooking Stanford Street. "Hey, man! What're you doing?" he called up. Carl didn't answer and retreated from view. As the man moved to mount the staircase, Carl walked deeper onto the roof, away from the edge. He stopped and turned again. Then he ran toward the edge—and kept going. He landed headfirst thirty-six feet below, on the sidewalk next to the church, his four-year battle with drug addiction and failed dreams quieted at last.

Carl's family—including his youngest sister, coauthor Amy Alexander—never expected that he would kill himself. Almost two decades passed before his mother and three younger siblings were able to assess Carl's decision with any degree of emotional detachment. In 1979, paralyzed by shame and guilt, they sought to honor their lost son and brother in the only way they knew how—by moving beyond the pain of his suicide with a quiet resolve to "get on with their lives." At the time and place of his death—the San Francisco Bay Area in the twilight of the Age of Aquarius—suicide did not seem a plausible result after the many minefields that they had watched Carl traverse. "Cowardly" is how Eric Fermon, Carl's younger brother, described the suicide at the time. And while Eric stood alone in expressing his anger at Carl's death, other family members shared Eric's sense of shame and confusion.

No one in their large circle of friends and relations had ever killed themselves. The only other black American they were aware of who had taken his own life was a promising pop singer, Donny Hathaway, who killed himself by leaping from the fifteenth floor of a Manhattan hotel just a month earlier, in January of 1979. Media reports of Hathaway's suicide mentioned the singer's "battle with depression" but provided few other details. Following Carl's death, the term "depression"–meaning an emotional state widely regarded by mental health professionals as a surefire indicator of a potential for suicidal thinking–did not occur to any of his survivors.

Did the suicide of Donny Hathaway, a rising star who'd had a handful of Top 40 hits in the 1970s, influence Carl's decision to leap from the roof of Star Bethel? Carl's family did not discuss the possibility. They knew that he had experienced several disappointments over the course of his young life. At the same time, they had seen in him a determination to make the best of his opportunities.

An average student throughout his years in high school, Carl had applied to the very selective Berkeley campus of the University of California during his senior year, through the university's equal opportunity program. Although he attributed his subsequent rejection to favoritism on the part of the program's coordinator–a Latino administrator whom he believed reserved his recommendations for a handful of Latino students from Wilson High–Carl's family members could not be sure of the accuracy of this belief, and Carl himself didn't seem unduly resentful of his failure to gain entry to Berkeley. Rather than attend college, he decided to go to work.

Indeed, throughout his teens, Carl had held down an after-school job at a day care center in San Francisco's Potrero Hill neighborhood. His three younger siblings attended the center, and administrators there had offered him a job as an aide when he was only fourteen, because they saw him as a responsible and conscientious young man. After he failed to get into Berkeley, the child care center's director arranged for Carl to interview for a job at Chevron in the East Bay, where her son worked as a supervisor.

For the next few years, Carl traveled each day from San Francisco to a big refinery in Richmond, on a hillside northeast of Oakland, where he donned a hard hat and monitored a series of valves and fixtures in his job as a chemical operator.

During this period, he also attempted to become a police officer. In 1975 he took the entrance exam for the San Francisco Police Academy. To his younger brother Eric, Carl explained that he saw himself as a good candidate for "special agent" in the S.F.P.D.'s elite corps. Eric wasn't sure what that might entail, but he watched as his older brother studied long and hard. When Carl failed to pass the exam (no one in his family was sure whether it was the written, oral, or physical part of the battery of tests that had been his undoing), once again he didn't seem to take the rejection too hard. What his family members didn't know at the time was that Carl may have been turned down by the academy because of a 1973 arrest for possessing a small amount of marijuana.

Later that same year, a male cousin that the family hadn't seen in decades came to visit, and attended a neighborhood party with Carl. During this visit, Carl, who had experimented with marijuana while in high school, got his first taste of heroin. At the time, he seemed to be happily dedicated to his work at Chevron. He'd moved out of his mother's house in San Francisco and traded in his rickety old Valiant for a gleaming black shark-shaped Dodge Charger.

As he became addicted to heroin, however, his life began to unravel. His supervisors at Chevron, alarmed by his erratic behavior, pulled him off the job and enrolled him in a drug rehabilitation service run by their employee assistance program. He completed the sixty-day program and returned to work but fell back into drug use within a year. When his supervisors again noticed telltale signs of heroin use they fired him. Without a steady job, Carl returned home to live with his family and enrolled in another drug rehabilitation program.

By 1977, Carl had completed half a dozen detoxification and rehabilitation programs, only to return to heroin use after each stint.

He became increasingly frustrated with his inability to quit using drugs or hold down a job, and his mental health began to deteriorate. At some point in 1977, he became convinced that a former classmate and sometime drug-using pal was responsible for the downward spiral his life seemed to be taking. He walked to the young man's house in San Francisco, broke in, and waited several hours for the former friend to return from work. When the young man got home, Carl surprised him in his darkened living room and beat him bloody with a length of pipe. It was a violent, irrational act, and out of character for a twenty-three-year-old man who had theretofore been a passive, easygoing individual. He served twenty-two days in the San Francisco City and County Jail for the assault, after which the district attorney, at the behest of Carl's mother, ordered him sent to a state psychiatric hospital.

For five months in 1977, Carl underwent drug counseling, anger management sessions, and psychiatric treatment at Atascadero State Hospital, on California's central coast. There staff doctors diagnosed him as having a "chronic, undifferentiated" type of schizophrenia and recommended that he begin taking Haldol, a psychotropic medication. After his release, Carl returned to live with his mother and three younger siblings in San Francisco. For a time he attended regular drug counseling sessions and seemed to stay away from heroin; by late 1978, however, his behavior at home had become disruptive. He stopped attending drug treatment programs and refused to take his medication. His mother, concerned for the well-being of her three school-aged children, asked Carl to leave. "Where do you expect me to live?" he asked her during a tense conversation in the autumn of 1978. "On a park bench? I don't have anywhere to go—it's not feasible to kick me out!"

Unmarried and hardworking, Carl's mother had reached the end of her resources in terms of her son's addiction. He had never known his father, but in the past that had not seemed to trouble him. Hazel had hoped that the months at Atascadero might return Carl to a healthy course; when he relapsed she was at a loss. For much of his young life, Carl's cousins and uncles had served as male role models, and his mother suggested he find a place to live with one of them, in the East Bay. One of the cousins, Lloyd Richardson, arranged for Carl to stay in the apartment he shared with his mother, Sara. It was from their front door near San Pablo Avenue that Carl walked to the fire escape at Star Bethel.

In a front-page story about Carl's suicide that appeared in the *Oakland Tribune* on March 12, 1979, a reporter attributed the young man's death to despair over his fight with drug addiction and his inability to hold a job. The *Tribune* account was accurate—but it was far from the whole story. "I knew something was riding him," Michael Carse recalled some twenty years later. "I don't know if you'd call it depression, but he was definitely being torn up by something."

During the last months of his life, as his mental health deteriorated and his drug abuse increased, Carl had begun to confide in his older cousin Michael. He expressed frustration about not being able to hold a job and sometimes railed at "the system" that seemed to be keeping him down. Raised in an integrated community, he never singled out any particular white person as contributing to his troubles, but in his mind the road to happiness seemed to be blocked by a powerful, white-dominated external force. He spoke of how circumstances seemed to be out of his control, and of how the cards appeared to be stacked against him. "He wasn't paranoid that someone was out to get him," Michael said. "He just seemed to feel that he faced a whole lot of obstacles and that 'the system' was set up in such a way that he couldn't get his life together. But he couldn't quite articulate what these things meant." In a curious twist of the process known as internalization, however, Carl's only act of lashing out against the perceived "system" had been carried out against a black man—the former classmate he'd attacked with a pipe in 1977.

Haunted by a looming sense of hopelessness and shame, Carl also shared his suicidal thoughts with Michael. At the time, Michael instructed Carl to "stay clean" and "stay strong." "I didn't know if he was serious, but I told him that killing himself was not the answer."

Just as Donny Hathaway's death had engendered shock and confusion within the black community nationwide—"We didn't think black people killed themselves" was a whispered refrain in many black households—so Carl's suicide provoked grief, shame, and silent introspection among his friends and family in California. And in some cases that grief became destructive. Lloyd, Michael's younger brother and Carl's sometime "running buddy," was not Carl's closest confidant, and he had been unable to stop Carl from leaving the apartment on the morning of his death. After his cousin's suicide, Lloyd slipped into a life of heavy drinking and drug abuse. Since that cold morning in 1979 when police officers brought him to the grim spot beside the church to identify Carl's broken body, Lloyd has lived on the streets of Oakland and Berkeley, panhandling and hustling for money to support his habits. His sister, Anita Carse, a nurse and another of Carl's older cousins, believes that Lloyd is engaged in a slow, determined suicide attempt of his own.

For a time following Carl's death, the violence and suddenness of his act pushed aside any consideration of the larger psychological and societal questions raised by his mental illness and his suicide. The same shame, guilt, and sadness endured by all suicide survivors—black, brown, or white; low-income or middle-class—were magnified in a family where a long tradition of education and work had always seemed to be the key to healthy, successful living. Moreover, no one had ever looked upon the uncles who drank too much or the young cousins who fell into drug abuse as possibly engaging in suicidal actions, forms of "slow suicide" manifested by chronic life-threatening behaviors.

"Work was the goal," said Anita Carse, who has spent a lot of time over the past twenty years trying to put Carl's predicament–and Lloyd's–into context. "Even if you worked yourself to death, what mattered most to our parents and grandparents was a strong work ethic. The drinking, drug abuse, and other health problems were overlooked as long as you went to work every day."

Carl's family had no point of reference for what had happened to him, and what little they knew about Hathaway's high-profile suicide did not prevent them from feeling alone in their shame and confusion. Since that brisk morning in 1979 they have borne in silence their grief and shame and their frustrating inability to answer so many key questions about Carl's death. Did the mental health care community fail Carl? Why did he keep returning to drugs despite completing numerous treatment and rehabilitation programs? Had schizophrenia made him completely irrational? What was it about his life that made living it so unbearable? Was it cowardly of him to kill himself rather than continue trying to cope with his problems?

During the same time period, the 1970s, countless other African-American families with middle-class goals, values, and aspirations were faced with a similarly devastating situation and a similar set of questions.

The troubled life and premature death of Kenneth Poussaint, an older brother of coauthor Alvin Poussaint, shows many parallels with Carl Burton's. While Kenneth Poussaint died in 1975 from acute meningitis, his family is uncertain if he was using heroin at the time, and an examination of his life reveals the possibility that his willingness to engage in life-threatening behaviors also represented a slow form of suicide.

Whereas Carl leapt to his death in a sudden, single, violent act, Kenny chose a lingering but equally certain path. And throughout Kenny's years-long battle with mental illness and drug abuse, and his brushes with criminal activity, his relatives carried in silence their overwhelming grief, shame, and confusion. Like the members of Carl's family, they felt isolated in their sadness and frustration, unsure of where to turn or how to help Kenny as he struggled with his illness. Ironically, both young black men were self-destructing at a time when the Black Power and civil rights movements were thought by many to have secured new opportunities and brighter futures for African-Americans.

During the late 1950s and into the 1960s, Kenny had been an average student in the New York City public school system. One of eight children, he was athletic, witty, and gifted with an intuitive nature that made him a whiz at sports and card games. He wanted to follow his father into the printing business and attended a vocational high school to learn the trade. An outgoing young man, Kenny was also a leader among his peers in the East Harlem neighborhood where he lived.

His family members are not certain of the details, but somewhere along the way Kenny developed an addiction to heroin. By the time he turned eighteen—the year his mother died—his relationship with his father had become tense; his addiction was known to the family, and he had often been beseeched to give up drugs. Kenny was torn up about his mother's passing. He was an eighteen-year-old high school graduate and this was a turning point in his young life. He vowed to give up drugs as a tribute to his mother, and he did—at least for a while.

It was during this period of abstinence that his siblings first noticed signs of mental illness in Kenny. He talked of their mother constantly in the present tense, as if she still moved through the rooms of their East Harlem home. She had been a light-skinned woman, and after her death, Kenny, who boasted a coffee-colored complexion, began washing his hands and face obsessively, saying, "If I keep washing, I'll become as white as Momma." He began describing his younger brother, Alvin, as being "white, like Momma," even though Alvin's complexion was the same coffee tone as his. He spun wildly paranoid, delusional stories, and in one harrowing incident threatened other members of the family with physical harm.

Finally Kenny locked himself in his bedroom and refused to let anyone else come in, saying he would "destroy" them if they did. Hours later he allowed Alvin, with whom he shared the room, to enter. When the police came to the home, Kenny begged his family not to let them take him away, and they sought to reassure him as the officers restrained him. Kenny was taken to Bellevue's psychiatric unit, where he was put in a straitjacket. Later he was transferred to Creedmore State Hospital, where psychiatrists diagnosed him as a paranoid schizophrenic.

Over the next year, Kenneth Poussaint was confined in the state mental hospital and treated with a combination of medications and insulin shock therapy. The latter treatment had been developed in the 1930s, following observations by psychiatrists that schizophrenic patients who for some reason lapsed into a coma later showed improvement in their mental status: doctors induced comas in such patients by injecting them with insulin, producing a hypoglycemic (low blood sugar) coma which was terminated after a period of fifteen minutes to an hour by a sugar injection. These induced comas were terrifying for Kenny, and he only gradually improved with the help of medications. In general, the effectiveness of insulin coma therapy was difficult to evaluate at best, and it was already falling into disuse in the 1950s and 1960s, as new antipsychotic drugs became available. The quality of Kenny's treatment was suspect, but the family was unsure of how to challenge the doctors about the level of care he received.

After his release, Kenny returned to East Harlem and the family home. Within two weeks he had succumbed to the lure of heroin once again. His family members saw him high and knew that he was caught up again in a life that included petty thefts and other criminal pursuits carried out to support his drug addiction. During this period, Alvin was sharing a room at home with Kenny while studying at Columbia University, and sometimes late at night he saw Kenny prepare and shoot drugs.

On several occasions he awoke to find his brother lying unconscious on the floor with a needle dangling from his arm. At these times Alvin feared that Kenny would die from an overdose; he began to wonder, in fact, if his brother would one day commit suicide this way.

Over the next few years, Kenneth Poussaint was arrested for petty, nonviolent crimes numerous times, and he served several sentences in prison on Rikers Island in New York. During this period he lost touch with his family.

When he resurfaced in East Harlem in the early 1970s, Kenny was a changed man. He told his family that he had entered a drug treatment program. Their contact with Kenny thereafter was sporadic, but when they did see him he seemed to waver between participation in various therapeutic methadone programs and periodic returns to intravenous heroin abuse.

For a time Kenny lived in a rented room and held down a job as a clerk in the county health department. His old friends and family, during their limited encounters with him, encouraged him to stay on course. For several years Kenny seemed to be doing well and enjoying the most stable period of his adult life; no one saw any signs of depression or serious problems in his social or work life.

To the Poussaint family, Kenny no longer showed symptoms of the mental illness that had surfaced in his late teens, but neither did his life appear to be completely stable. When they learned that he had contracted meningitis, some of his relatives wondered whether he was off heroin or had contracted the illness by injecting himself with a contaminated needle. (A friend later reported that he was still shooting heroin.) One of the risks of using dirty needles–a common practice among intravenous drug users–is bacterial contamination injected directly into the bloodstream, which may quickly infect the membranes of the brain; a rapidly progressing meningitis develops that is often fatal. (Today, of course, besides bacterial infections, addicts are at high risk for contracting HIV/AIDS when sharing contaminated needles.)

In 1975, Kenny Poussaint died in the emergency room at Harlem Hospital at age forty-two, his vital organs defeated by years of drug abuse and a final fatal physical illness.

Like Carl Burton's family members, the Poussaint family found that their love for Kenny was, over the years, tempered by shame, and in both cases that shame was marked by frustration and anger at a loved one's seemingly willful self-destructive behavior. Amid their individual progress, their gradual climb into the great American middle class, the families of Kenneth Poussaint and Carl Burton still mourn their loss, and the fact that, for all their promise, these two young men died in so much pain is a weighty burden that they continue to bear.

Now, some twenty years later–as more instances of black Americans struggling with mental health problems become public and the rate of suicide among black people shows a slow, steady increase–Carl's and Kenny's surviving family members find little consolation in realizing that they are not alone. And they still struggle to make sense of it all.

Consequently we hope that this book will help African-Americans better understand and seek help for relatives and friends who manifest mental disorders and self-destructive behaviors.

Alvin F. Poussaint, M.D.
Amy Alexander
Boston, Massachusetts
January, 2000

Introduction

Posttraumatic Slavery Syndrome

The short, turbulent lives and premature deaths of Carl Burton and Kenneth Poussaint raise urgent questions about the overlooked connections between racial oppression, hopelessness, self-hatred, economics, stress, and the patterns of self-destructive behavior exhibited by some black Americans. And, most important, their stories provide a chilling glimpse into the taboo subject of black mental health and the increasing rates of suicide among African-Americans.

On several levels, Carl Burton and Kenneth Poussaint fit the profile of what has become a growing phenomenon in the United States since the late 1970s: young blacks who self-destruct. For example, among black youths aged fifteen to nineteen, the rate of suicide has more than doubled since 1980, rising from 3.6 to 8.1 deaths per 100,000 in 1996. For African-Americans between the ages of fifteen and twenty-four, suicide is now the third leading cause of death, behind homicides and accidents, according to the United States Centers for Disease Control and Prevention.[1] The suicide rate among blacks is still below that of whites, and within a given year the suicides of black males outnumber those of black females, but the increase in black suicides between the late 1970s and the 1990s is dramatic.

And while it falls far below the radar of national public consciousness, the growing number of African-American suicides might be viewed as a bellwether for our society at the beginning of this century. Although we don't have all the answers to this frightening development, in this book we intend to examine some of its possible causes.

Inspired by the deaths of our respective siblings, our challenge is to shed long overdue light on the complicated social, historical, and psychological elements behind the troubling increase in dangerous lifestyles and suicide among black Americans. We are aware that Kenneth Poussaint and Carl Burton cannot possibly stand as exact mirrors of every black person who has self-destructed during the past twenty years; nevertheless, we have identified several important threads in their experiences that are relevant to the suicides of thousands of African-Americans in recent years–and to the state of our society as a whole.

Both Carl Burton and Kenneth Poussaint began experimenting with drugs at an early age. Both young men had contact with the criminal justice system and had served time for crimes related to their addictions. Both were diagnosed with mental illnesses, yet they declined to stay on a medication schedule; indeed, their drug abuse might possibly be seen as an attempt at self-medication. Both young men became increasingly isolated from their families while family members struggled to find effective means of helping them. Both expressed, within their respective forms of mental illness, a pre-occupation with the influence that they believed whites, and a white-dominated "system," held over their lives. And both young men, caught in a cycle of drug abuse, criminal activity, and self-loathing, grew to devalue themselves to such a degree that an early death was not discounted as an alternative to the struggle that living had become.

For their respective family members, the aftermath of the deaths of Carl Burton and Kenneth Poussaint was marked by anguish, introspection, and a determined resolve to move forward with their own lives.

The survivors did not immediately blame the mental health care community for its failure to prevent, or at least predict, the premature deaths of their loved ones. In reality, attempting to place such blame would have been futile: historically, the nation's medical establishment has been as stumped by the suicide conundrum as is the lay community. Indeed, coauthor Alvin Poussaint, a veteran psychiatrist, has been on the other side of the treatment equation and has experienced firsthand the difficulty of trying to stop someone who decides to take his or her own life.

At the same time, the diagnostic models–the suicide "warning signs" established and accepted by mental health care policymakers nationwide over the past fifty years–have not always been effective in addressing the unique mental health concerns of black Americans. Further, the well-documented high rate of homicide among blacks might be viewed as evidence of a peculiar kind of communal self-hatred, an especially virulent form of anger, self-loathing, and lost hope that leads to a devaluation of the lives of fellow blacks; and that same self-hatred may also lead to a devaluation of self, which can result in life-threatening, self-destructive, or suicidal behavior.

Similar dynamics of self-devaluation and hopelessness may account, in part, for the high rates of alcoholism and drug addiction among black people in this society.

Any attempt to assess this possibility must include an understanding of how American history continues to influence the lives of blacks. The hopelessness and cynicism currently felt by many African-Americans more than a century after the end of slavery did not develop in a vacuum.

The young black male who takes up a firearm and engages an opponent in a confrontation, for instance, has made a decision to put his life on the line. Consciously or not, such a youth sees violence carried out in the name of "respect" as an acceptable way of dying. Often faced with the message that their lives are not valued in American society, young blacks may internalize their despair—or externalize it. The hard-living man or woman knows that promiscuity, excessive drinking, drug use, and tobacco smoking all put one's health at serious risk, yet many continue to engage in these behaviors, knowing but choosing to ignore the fact that such behavior may bring about an early death.

Complicating the philosophical question of why any individual might choose to engage in self-destructive behavior is the unmistakable resistance that many blacks have to seeking assistance from the medical community. This resistance, which includes a strong disinclination to seek mental health care, can be traced to a long and sullied track record where blacks and the American medical and psychiatric/psychological establishments are concerned.

Until the late 1960s, many hospitals and health care clinics throughout the South were segregated institutions where blacks received little or inferior care, if any, and less blatant de facto discrimination existed in the North as well. Because blacks were routinely refused acceptance at many hospitals, they were unable to receive early preventive care for treatable illnesses and conditions. Due to segregation and discrimination, in the North as well as in the South, blacks often died from treatable diseases and illnesses. Further, many white doctors, nurses, and other staff at health care institutions of all kinds were openly racist, leaving blacks with no reason to trust a system that demonstrated little regard for the value of a black life.

The mistreatment that African-Americans were often exposed to during their limited contact with the health care establishment included instances of unconsenting blacks being used as research subjects in dangerous experiments; the infamous case in which white government doctors directed syphilis experiments on unwitting black patients through the Tuskegee Institute during the 1930s and 1940s is but the best-known example among many.

This lack of regard and dehumanizing treatment has fostered distrust, even a sense of paranoia and fear; some black Americans, for example, say that they believe that the virus that causes AIDS was deliberately introduced by whites to decimate the African-American and African populations. Conspiracy theories aside, only in the past few years has the predominantly white health care system begun to acknowledge what the comparatively small number of black health care professionals and their allies have long known about the black community nationwide.

The well-documented high rates of heart disease, hypertension, and other stress-related illnesses found in African-Americans are traceable in part to social factors, including most prominently the long history of blacks being required to endure racism, poverty, discrimination, and the lack of adequate health services—including mental health care—in America.

The persistent presence of racism, despite the significant legal, social, and political progress made during the last half of the twentieth century, has created a physiological risk for black people that is virtually unknown to white Americans. We call this posttraumatic slavery syndrome. Specifically, a culture of oppression, the byproduct of this nation's development, has taken a tremendous toll on the minds and bodies of black people. We see the increasing rates of black suicide in the United States—and the remarkable fact that blacks comprise less than 13 percent of the U.S. population but represent the overwhelming majority of those doing time in the nation's prisons for violent or drug-related crimes—as part and parcel of that oppression. Yet in the realm of mental health, where blacks' rates of clinical illness and depression approach those of whites, the concerns of blacks have received a fraction of the attention accorded to those of whites by those in the research, policy, and political communities who hold the power to address these issues.

A dearth of nonwhite mental health clinicians (a shortage that may also be traced to racism, specifically to limited access to higher education afforded blacks, Latinos, and other minority groups throughout much of U.S. history) has resulted in a significant gap in understanding between the medical establishment and ethnic minorities in America.

For example, in many instances, white mental health practitioners–conditioned by years of cultural stereotypes depicting blacks as leading emotionally uncomplicated lives–have trouble acknowledging depression in black Americans. Consequently, severe clinical depression is often underdiagnosed among black Americans.

At the same time, these clinicians–also conditioned by equally persistent images of blacks (males in particular) as being dangerous, threatening, and prone to paranoia–tend to overdiagnose schizophrenia among blacks. Compounding matters, most clinicians find it difficult to accurately assess the risk of suicide among schizophrenic patients, particularly since those suffering from disorders now believed to involve chemical imbalances (manic-depressive illness, severe depression, and schizophrenia) are often given to delusions and hallucinations. As a rule of thumb, mental health clinicians have been trained to look upon severely depressed patients as likely to provide early warning signs of suicidal thinking, but schizophrenic patients are not as likely to present clearly definable suicidal intention. Of course, even in severely depressed individuals, it is not always easy to predict or prevent suicide.

Among black Americans, who in many instances have become accustomed to downplaying outward signs of depression or suicidal thinking, mental health practitioners must be prepared to employ a uniquely personal and sensitive approach to assessment and treatment. For black Americans, the "language of depression" often varies from that which a white interviewer might be accustomed to recognizing: describing oneself as having "the blues" or "the aching misery," or as "being down" may indicate a severe depression that slips past an unsophisticated practitioner. And the fact that many black Americans do not seek help from mental health clinicians, or have been put off by previous contacts with insensitive ones, creates an access dilemma which makes the medical practitioner's role all the more crucial. Even when a black American makes it as far as an initial consultation, there is no guarantee that the health care practitioner will be able to address his or her particular experience and succeed in pulling the patient back from the brink.

Many years ago, a middle-aged black man sought counseling from coauthor Alvin Poussaint. He expressed suicidal feelings and rage that his wife had recently left him. Upset and visibly agitated at the beginning of the session, he settled down and eventually allowed that he did not really wish to end his life. Following the session, with permission and as a precaution, Poussaint informed one of the patient's close friends to keep watch on him; the friend reported to Poussaint later that same evening that the man seemed to be doing well.

When the patient failed to show up for his next scheduled session the following morning, Poussaint became concerned; shortly thereafter, the friend phoned to tell him that the man had killed himself. Poussaint was devastated but realized that either this patient had been determined to end his life and deliberately misled Poussaint as well as his friend, or he had killed himself impulsively in a moment of renewed anger and despair.

Overall, the intricacies of an individual's despair are a mystery. What is certain, however, is the need for mental health practitioners to be as aware as possible of specific cultural factors underlying the surface of a patient's immediate concerns. To "take the extra step" with African-American patients may require a focused understanding of the special burdens that many blacks carry.

Twenty years ago, the rate of suicide among white youths was more than double that of blacks, but that gap has now narrowed to 42 percent, according to the Centers for Disease Control and Prevention (CDC).[2] While the sudden suicide of Carl Burton and the slower self-destruction of Kenneth Poussaint predate the most recent CDC figures, their stories represent a larger trend now facing black Americans—the troubling possibility that three centuries' worth of communal strength and individual self-preservation is eroding. The rise in self-destructive behaviors among blacks—unlike the high incidence of "black crime"—has received little in-depth examination from the nation's policymakers.

Only in the past few years has public consciousness been alerted to this unhappy subject, and in these media-saturated times, that attention has been aroused in ways that lend little insight or helpful analysis for realistically examining the causes behind it.

Since the early 1990s, the popular press has reported intermittently on cases of "suicide by cop," sometimes referred to as victim-precipitated homicide, a situation in which a distraught individual (usually male, and in a few high-profile instances, a black male) arms himself and intentionally goads law enforcement officials into shooting him. Meanwhile, the criminal justice system now houses more black men than do the nation's colleges, with an estimated one in four African-American males of voting age falling under some kind of court supervision or incarceration.

Mainstream media examinations of suicide among blacks have uniformly lacked intelligent, informed discussions of the possible motivations for its increase. For example, a March 20, 1998, *New York Times* front-page story speculated, with no research support, that middle-class black youths were killing themselves in greater numbers out of disillusionment with their "new affluence"; in fact, the 1998 CDC report chronicling the rise in black suicide did not provide a breakdown by income or education level, yet a researcher's comment to the *Times* on the possibility of middle-class angst as the primary motivation for the increase became the guiding "spin" of the *Times* story. Such speculative coverage lends an air of absolutism to an area of study that is woefully incomplete. In short, demographic information that would be helpful in understanding black suicide is missing from the government's arsenal of resources.

Also missing from the recent limited public discussion of the rise in black suicide are realistic assessments of the possible motivations for the increase. The proliferation of guns, violence, and drugs, the breakdown of the extended family structure, involvement in the criminal justice system, and a pervasive sense of hopelessness among young people in many black communities are important but largely overlooked. These factors, combined with a misguided view held by some young black males of what constitutes "respect," could very well represent a formula that will inevitably lead to more and more blacks bringing their lives to a premature end.

At the same time, while from San Francisco to Atlanta growing numbers of black American families of every income and education level struggle to cope with loved ones who have serious mental health problems, the dominant reaction of many black families is disbelief that a black person would commit suicide as a way of ending their earthly troubles. Significantly, the role of religion is rarely questioned, although it might be relevant that throughout the more than three-hundred-year history of black people in the United States, Christian African-Americans begin as children to absorb the teaching that strife and tribulation here on earth will be redeemed by the sweetness of a heavenly afterlife. At the same time, many black churches have for decades preached on the "sin" of taking one's own life, an archaic outlook that may contribute to the wall of secrecy that continues to prevent African-Americans from engaging in open discussions about family members who struggle with depression or self-destructive behaviors. Their stories, relayed in whispers and with lots of heart but little understanding, are made up of many elements, their contours defined by many elusive factors.

We believe that all of these elements, particularly the obvious but rarely studied components like persistent stress and despair among blacks because of racism and the legacy of slavery, must be thoroughly examined before we can know whether Carl Burton and Kenneth Poussaint were exceptions or prototypes. Obviously, many negative conditions have existed in black communities for centuries—including drugs, racial discrimination, firearms, and despair. We propose that never before has their particular combination existed in such a high-stakes, powder-keg social environment, at a time in which racism often bears a seemingly benign, difficult to recognize face.

But in our collective history as a nation, with the exception of Native Americans, no other population besides blacks has had to struggle harder for self-preservation, to withstand the hardships and low blows that life can offer. The need to bear up under centuries of cruel treatment has made black Americans in some ways particularly resilient—and in some ways reluctant to admit personal vulnerabilities, especially where mental illness is concerned.

What were the coping mechanisms that allowed black people to endure centuries of brutality and servitude without being psychologically and socially destroyed? Do these coping skills exist in black America in the 1990s? How do we know that the extraordinarily high rates of lifestyle-related health problems, homicide, drug abuse, and other destructive behaviors in black America are not, in fact, some expression of suicide? Scant official research exists in this area, and what studies do exist have been done with inadequate or outdated methodologies, which makes their findings questionable at best.

In this book, we will examine accepted mental health care concepts and practices in order to explore anew the complicated issues of modern African-American suicide and related mental health issues.

We will analyze the history of blacks and the mental health care community in the United States, and take a hard look at the real-life subtexts, personal impact on individuals, and long-term implications of the rise in black suicide.

In this context, we will offer recommendations for curbing self-destructive behaviors among black people, and suggest ways to improve the black community's access to mental health services. Along with our own personal experience of the living angst that is the aftermath of suicide, the authors share a combined total of fifty years of observation and involvement with black health care issues.

We believe that a national discussion about suicide, mental health issues, and access to health care in minority communities is long overdue. As a black psychiatrist and black journalist respectively, we have each encountered psychological aspects of the African-American experience that have been overlooked by much of the public and by policymakers—several centuries' worth of burdensome psychic baggage, if you will—which require honest analysis if blacks are to flourish in the twenty-first century. *Lay My Burden Down* is an effort to raise our collective awareness about the mental health needs of millions of underserved Americans. Through the memories and experiences of suicide survivors, historians, and mental health care experts, we hope to begin a productive discussion that will be the first step in a long, difficult, and necessary national discourse.

1

"He Didn't Seem Depressed"

Faces behind the Numbers

The suicide or self-destruction of a loved one is traumatic for those who are left behind. Extending across ethnic, class, and gender lines, suicide leaves an emotional weight on surviving family members and friends that can be devastating, and the stigma attached to suicide is especially great for African-Americans. The early deaths of our brothers, Kenneth Poussaint and Carl Burton, were the endgame of their own experiences, unique in their respective ways and to the times in which they lived. Still, it is not a contradiction to argue that the premature deaths of both men showed patterns that we believe are fairly common among black suicides, including the emotional after-effects felt by their survivors. Among the thousands of blacks who committed suicide between the 1970s and the late 1990s, it is likely that several common traits exist, though obviously the specifics of each case differ.

To begin with, when an individual is moving toward a conscious decision to take his or her own life, clinical signs often precede the suicide attempt. Any person, young or old, suffering from a severe depression should be considered a potential self-murderer. Individuals who experience severe depression have a 15 percent lifetime risk of suicide, and schizophrenics have a 10 percent risk. Persons with impulsive, unstable, angry, and antisocial personalities also have a higher risk of suicide than the general population. In general, the more serious the mental symptoms, the graver the risk.[1] Ninety percent of completed suicides are committed by people suffering from some form of major psychiatric illness.[2]

Major symptoms of severe depression are profound sadness, a lack of pleasure and interest in previously enjoyable activities, feelings of hope-lessness, self-depreciation, guilt, tenseness, insomnia, rapid gain or loss of weight, fatigue, and physical agitation or a noticeable slowing down of movement. Some people may show increased bodily symptoms such as aches, pains, headaches, and gastrointestinal upsets, what an early-twentieth-century generation of Southern-born blacks might term the "aching misery." It is important to note that even patients suffering from mild depression, as well as those with a psychotic depression, may commit suicide, particularly after a severe loss or humiliation. In young people—especially in impulsive, severely angry, or psychotic individuals—acute depression following a severe life crisis should be cause for concern about suicidal potential.

Young blacks in particular are more likely to kill themselves after a con-frontation or perceived victimization by institutional authorities such as the police, the criminal justice system, school officials, the welfare depart-ment, or a landlord. A sense of hopelessness and feelings of shame because of unemployment, poverty, and/or seemingly unresolvable social problems will increase the likelihood of suicide, and even of homicide. Any person who has repeatedly stated that "life is not worth living" and has expressed a wish to die should be considered at severe risk. In the presence of depres-sion, other factors that may indicate an increased potential for suicide are a history of previous attempts, previous psychosis, suicide notes, chronic or acute illness, alcoholism, drug dependence, and the stresses that may ac-company homosexuality.

In the cases of the authors' brothers, there were clear risk factors for sui-cidal behaviors. They both abused drugs and showed evidence of previous psychosis accompanied by moderate amounts of depression. In addition, Amy Alexander's brother, Carl Burton, had suffered from humiliation and shame secondary to chronic underemployment and unemployment. Other traits they shared in common with other relatively young black male sui-cides include advancing age, social isolation, and loneliness. (Individuals from stable communities and supportive family situations are usually not as inclined to self-murder because of protective factors that have not been well understood or researched.)

Before we go forward with our focus on the black community, some information about suicide in general seems in order.

The U.S. *Surgeon General's Call to Action to Prevent Suicide*,[3] released in the summer of 1999 to herald an official government effort to address suicide and mental health problems, offered the following list of risk factors with which practitioners and laypeople should become familiar:

- previous suicide attempt
- mental disorders, particularly mood disorders such as depression and bipolar (manic-depressive) disorder
- co-occurring mental and alcohol and substance abuse disorders
- family history of suicide
- hopelessness
- impulsive and/or aggressive tendencies
- barriers to accessing mental health treatment
- relational (i.e., death or divorce), social, work, or financial loss
- physical illness
- easy access to lethal methods, especially guns
- unwillingness to seek help because of the stigma attached to mental and substance abuse disorders and/or suicidal thoughts
- influence of significant people–family members, celebrities, peers–who have died by suicide, both through direct personal contact or inappropriate media representations
- cultural and religious beliefs–for instance, the belief that suicide is a noble resolution of a personal dilemma
- local epidemics of suicide that have a contagious influence
- isolation, a feeling of being cut off from other people

The *Surgeon General's Call* also summarized "best practice" recommendations for medical and mental health professionals.

The usual treatment of the suicidal patient may involve individual psychotherapy, group therapy, antidepressant drugs, and/or electric shock therapy. Acutely suicidal patients should always be hospitalized for their own protection. Generally, when suicide is a clear possibility patients should be referred to a mental health facility or the nearest hospital emergency room, most of which have psychiatrists on staff.

Physicians should not hesitate to discuss suicide with patients who appear depressed or who they suspect might be considering suicide. A simple question such as, Have you thought of killing yourself? may provide life-saving information. There is no evidence that raising the question of suicide harms the patient or will precipitate a suicide attempt.

At the same time, doctors should be careful about prescribing barbiturates and other sedatives to depressed or impulsive patients. Alcoholics and drug addicts are particularly likely to take "accidental" drug overdoses that result in death. Physicians should avoid the abrupt withdrawal of antidepressants and other medications from which depressed patients receive some relief of symptoms, because a deepening of depression will increase the suicide risk.

In addition, doctors should inquire about the availability of firearms in the home, or medicines that can be easily taken to produce a fatal overdose. Working with family members to have guns and dangerous medications secured or discarded should be an important responsibility of the treating clinician.

A suicidal person who is to be hospitalized should not be permitted to return home or carry out any chores after the hospitalization decision has been made, but should be admitted quickly and with the necessary precautions.

In the final analysis, predicting suicide in a particular individual is difficult. There is no foolproof constellation of predictors; psychological testing and clinical evaluations are not sensitive or accurate enough. And unfortunately there is no specific biological test for markers that would predict the likelihood of an imminent suicide attempt in a particular individual. However, people with certain mental disorders, such as manic-depressive illness, clinical depression, schizophrenia, or severe anxiety (panic attack) disorders, are at greater lifelong risk. The same is true for substance abusers, including alcoholics. And there should be particular concern for those who have made previous suicide attempts or who express suicidal thoughts.

One of the most successful strategies for curbing suicide has been the establishment of prevention centers throughout the country, which began in 1958. These centers can usually be reached by telephone hotlines during all hours of the day and night, and staff members are trained to persuade the caller to come in for an interview or accept a referral. After the situation is evaluated, the client is likely to receive some counseling or may be seen on a long-term basis by a caseworker, psychologist, or psychiatrist, or immediate hospitalization may be arranged. In cases of attempted suicide, the entire family must often become involved to help the member in distress; in fact, it may be that something gone awry in the family environment has precipitated the suicide attempt. If a suicide hotline is not available in a particular community, friends or family members who are worried about an individual should call a physician, clinic, or hospital for help.

The hidden-in-plain-sight aspect of depression and suicide is particularly acute among African-Americans.

"I think depression is probably the most deadly disease in the black community today," said John A. Wilson, chairman of the District of Columbia Council, speaking about mental health issues in a 1993 talk to local mental health professionals.

"I think that more people are dying of depression," he continued, "than are dying of AIDS, heart trouble, high blood pressure, anything else, simply because . . . depression brings on all of those diseases." A few days after his talk, in which he also referred to his own twenty-year bout with depression, Wilson, a veteran black District politician, hanged himself in the basement of his southwest D.C. home. His suicide, according to the *Washington Post,* saddened his closest friends and family members, who were well aware of the councilman's long battle with depression, and it shocked his coworkers and constituents, who did not know how intense his struggle with his illness had been. Unfortunately, Wilson's dramatic death in the capital of the nation failed to spark a widespread public awakening to the urgency of mental health issues from within or outside the black community.

The fundamental challenge of identifying and addressing the causal factors of black suicide lies in overcoming the recondite nature of the subject within the black community and the stigma attached to it, which is stubborn and strong.

The pronounced feelings of shame, guilt, and confusion that surround suicide in general lead to a high degree of denial among friends and family members of blacks who take their own lives, and foster an unwillingness to acknowledge the self-determination that makes suicide possible. This denial of suicide as a self-propelled act makes open discussion of issues and individual cases especially difficult in the black community.

The defensive mechanisms that have allowed this denial to become embedded in the black psyche are in many ways understandable. As members of a population conditioned by centuries of racial discrimination to cope with tribulations, many black Americans view suicide as a sinful and cowardly response to the pressures of living, a sign of personal weakness that is to be avoided at all costs. Suffering through "the blues" is seen as an expected rite of passage for most black Americans, and many show a relatively high level of tolerance for methods of "getting by" which might otherwise be viewed as self-destructive. An additional barrier to recognizing the importance of seeking professional treatment for a wide range of personal problems is the fact that an individual who reaches out for help or counseling from anyone other than close family, a friend, or a pastor might be seen by the larger community as showing signs of weakness or, even worse, as "putting his business in the street."

We believe, however, that the realities of modern life have begun to undermine the historic adaptations, the coping strategies, that are part of African-American culture. The internal strength which allowed blacks to endure centuries of hardships has, it seems to us, morphed over the decades into a form of stoicism that provides little room for acknowledging and addressing mental health problems.

Combined with the self-medicating practices of some blacks—alcohol and drug abuse may be fueled by frustration over poverty, discrimination, and racism—this stolid posture eventually works against an individual, shutting him or her off from nondestructive alternatives that might provide relief from life's stresses and pain.

If suicide is anathema to the American doctrine of strength in the face of adversity, it is doubly antithetical to the black experience and to the accepted burden of bearing up under monumentally difficult circumstances, as encoded in African-American work songs, spirituals, and the blues.

Any statistical analyses of black suicide, therefore, is virtually meaningless without considering the cultural and historic context of an individual's particular circumstances. High-profile suicides, such as those of D.C. councilman John Wilson in 1993 and pop singer Donny Hathaway during the late 1970s, flicker in the media momentarily before fading from view. But there is no time in the quick flash of celebrity news coverage for analysis, reflection, or discussion which might lead to prevention, give understanding and solace to survivors, or increase public awareness about suicides in black households.

We believe that these are important concerns. In order to emphasize the real-world impact of suicide on black Americans, we will add to our earlier look at our brothers' cases the stories of three individuals who also took their own lives: a twenty-six-year-old woman from Illinois, a sixteen-year-old boy from Colorado, and a six-year-old girl from Florida.

The first two cases come to us from family members who attended the conference on African-Americans and suicide sponsored by the National Organization for People of Color Against Suicide, held in Atlanta in February of 1999. The third case, that of the six-year-old girl in Florida, was recounted by her mother, siblings, police reports, and a social worker following the girl's death in 1993. Viewed independently, each of these stories is instructive about the varieties of pressures that come to bear on an individual, and of the many different ways in which individuals, absent skilled, sensitive professional assistance or familial or peer intervention, can negatively respond to those pressures. Taken together as a sample of the thousands of African-Americans who chose to end their own lives over the past thirty years, these stories are valuable pieces to an elusive psychosocial puzzle. If any universal lessons are to be found in them, perhaps the first is that the mental health care community must devise ways of reaching individuals from underrepresented groups, particularly those who may show few outward signs of being in grave psychological or emotional distress.

Michelle Jackson was in her early twenties when she first attempted suicide by swallowing a handful of antidepressant pills. In June 1984, at the age of twenty-six, she killed herself–or "completed suicide," in the parlance of some suicidologists–by slicing her wrists and overdosing on a relative's blood-pressure medication. Her death followed a period of several years during which she had grappled with symptoms of mental illness and an inability to communicate to her family members and clinical workers the exact nature of her perturbation.

"In the end, I think that she was just tired of it," says her sister Vanessa. "But for so many years, she had been misdiagnosed, and neither she nor my family had the language to describe what was happening to her."

Michelle Jackson was a middle child among six born to a working-class family in Springfield, Illinois. Vanessa Jackson, one of her younger sisters, is now a clinical social worker in Georgia. For Vanessa, her sister's story is a powerful example of how some blacks are failed by the medical and mental health communities—and of how well-meaning family members sometimes fail to acknowledge the severity of a loved one's mental distress. Denial on the part of individuals and institutions, Vanessa says, was a major obstacle to assessing and treating Michelle's illness.

Despite several attempts at outpatient therapy and at least five hospitalizations, Michelle Jackson never managed to connect with a mental health professional who might have helped her find the combination of medication and other treatments that would have allowed her to lead a productive life.

"I knew she was upset," Vanessa says. "But I had false hope that she wouldn't kill herself, because even though she once tried to overdose, she'd always said she was too afraid to ever hurt herself." More than fifteen years after her sister's suicide, Vanessa Jackson looks back and continues to wonder if she or others in her family could have done something to prevent it.

Michelle's suicide helped convince Vanessa to become a clinical social worker, and she now directs a mental health awareness initiative in Georgia. She says that her experience with her sister has made her "humble" before the African-American clients she encounters in her work. "There are so many questions facing blacks where mental health care is concerned. We need to know what the term 'well' means for us. We also need to ask who is defining these terms, and whether or not our particular experiences are being addressed. We need to begin remaking medical and mental health institutions in our own image." The journey that led Vanessa Jackson to raise these questions began with her sister's long struggle.

Michelle, nicknamed Mickey by her family members, was "a gentle person, a real peacekeeper," Vanessa recalls. She isn't sure of the timing of the onset of her sister's emotional distress and has only a hint of what precipitated Michelle's first psychiatric hospitalization. Michelle had enlisted in the U.S. Army after graduating from high school and was sent to South Carolina for training.

Two years into her tour of duty, in the early 1980s, something traumatic happened while Michelle was stationed in Kentucky. "We never figured out what it was," Vanessa says. "She just told me some years later that 'They really hurt me and I just can't talk about it.' She never explained who 'they' were, or what it was that had hurt her." The exact nature of Michelle's early treatment–she was flown from the army base in Kentucky to Walter Reed Hospital in Washington, D.C.–is unknown to her family members. According to Vanessa, the military never provided the family with her sister's diagnostic or treatment records: "We just know that when she came home, after being hospitalized for several months, she was numb."

Her family members didn't have the money to travel from Illinois to the nation's capital, so Michelle was alone during her time at Walter Reed. "While she was institutionalized that first time, we weren't able to visit her and it was a time of guilt for all of us," Vanessa says. In her estimation, Michelle did not quite recover her easygoing personality: "She never quite regrouped, never seemed to develop a sense of purpose." The years between Michelle's first hospitalization (which was voluntary) and her suicide were fraught with difficulties. She was treated with antidepressant medications, including lithium, and with electric shock treatment. She appeared to suffer from manic depression, alternating between periods (sometimes weeks) of being hyperactive, and periods (sometimes months) when she was barely able to leave the house.

For a time, Michelle lived with Vanessa, who observed her sister's dramatic mood swings at firsthand. "She went through a phase where she was really 'up,' really dynamic, wanting to shop all the time and go out. I used to joke and call her a 'party girl,'" Vanessa says. "But now I know it was part of a cycle." Inevitably, a deep low would follow these periods of accelerated activity. More than once, Michelle went to a local hospital and admitted herself. "The first time it happened, she was at McFarland Hospital, a state facility outside Springfield [Illinois]," Vanessa says. This was a frightening experience for the Jacksons, especially since Vanessa and her siblings had heard, from the time they were in grade school, that "crazy people" ended up at McFarland. "And suddenly, there we were, visiting my sister."

During that first visit, Vanessa was shocked by what she saw at the state-run psychiatric hospital: "It was a snake pit. There were all these people in a big room, a day room, just shuffling around. Now I know that look, it's called 'the Thorazine shuffle'"–a stiff-spastic gait that is a side effect of Thorazine-type antipsychotic medications. Also, a large percentage of the patients at the state hospital were black, which surprised Vanessa. "How come I didn't know that so many black people were ending up in these kinds of hospitals?" she wondered then.

Some in the Jackson family didn't take issue with the generally questionable state of the facilities where Michelle was treated, but they all knew that she was not improving. (It should be noted here that a sizable percentage of severely mentally ill patients do not respond to any form of treatment.) When they asked Michelle how she spent her days, she shrugged and said she played checkers or watched television.

The staff at the hospital was surly and poorly trained, in Vanessa's opinion. At least one of them displayed a cruel streak: "I was visiting one day, and I asked the nurse on duty in the day room for a pack of cards, so my sister and I could play. And when she handed them to me, she said, 'Well, you know it's not a full deck!' and then started laughing. . . . I couldn't believe it." But private institutions were too expensive, and anyway, they figured, they would never know whether Michelle would have fared better in a private facility: the time she had spent in a well-regarded military hospital had not seemed to help.

As heartbroken as they felt over the next several years, Michelle's family members were hard-pressed to sort through the various levels of treatment options, doctors, and facilities to find an appropriate "program" that reconciled with their limited finances. Michelle's symptoms disrupted their lives, and the tension this caused could become unbearable at times. Infighting occurred within the family, the by-product of stress and a sense of helplessness. "[For a while,] I began to focus on my mother's passivity and the denial of some of my other family members," Vanessa recalls. Eventually, a sense of fatalism set in, an unspoken acceptance that Michelle's situation was bad and not likely to improve.

And whereas Michelle had been involved in her treatment in the years following her first "breakdown," over time she lost the determination that she had shown earlier. "I think that after she had been hospitalized four or five times, she realized that she was a so-called chronic," says Vanessa.

Michelle had been "in the system" and was all too familiar with its shortcomings. After years of bouncing from clinics to day treatment programs to state hospitals, she lost faith that the doctors, pills, clinics, and counselors who represented that system could help her regain an even psychological keel.

In the late spring of 1984, Michelle Jackson returned to her parents' home after a weeks-long visit at McFarland. On the afternoon of June 3, 1984, Vanessa went clothes shopping, spent a few breezy hours in a park with a friend, and planned to stop by and see her sister that evening, to show her the fine black suit she had bought. "It was a beautiful day," she says. "I was feeling good, and I wanted to share it with my sister." A message from her mother awaited her on the answering machine at her apartment: "Mickey's hurt herself—I think you'd better come home." At that time, Vanessa was twenty-four years old and studying for a master's degree in social work. After that day, several years would pass before Vanessa felt emotionally able to resume her studies; her grief spiraled into depression, and she eventually went into psychotherapy in order to help her regain her footing.

On that warm spring afternoon, Vanessa went immediately to St. John's Hospital, thinking that her parents would drive Michelle there, as they had done in the past, and she would meet them and begin the long march through the drifts of red tape that was part of the nightmare of these visits. But none of her family turned up at St. John's. During the forty-five minutes that she waited at the hospital, Vanessa phoned her parents several times and got a busy signal. As she pulled up in front of their modest house, she saw the bright lights of emergency medical services vehicles flashing along the tree-lined street.

A local minister greeted her on the walkway. "What the hell is *this?*" she remembers thinking. The minister tried to console her but she pushed him away angrily. "The church wants us to pray on everything, yet all the praying in the world never did take care of my sister," she thought. (Anger at the loss of the person one loves is often among the first emotions experienced in a grief reaction.) Michelle had died a few hours earlier, after slipping quietly into one of the bathrooms at her parents' house and taking her own life.

Their father was not at home, and when Vanessa reached him by phone at his work, she cried hard and told him that she needed him. "When he got home I just ran and clung to him. He's not very demonstrative, but I needed him to comfort me, and he did."

For the first month following Michelle's suicide, Vanessa's father refused to sleep inside the house where Michelle had died. "He'd sleep in his van, parked in front of the house," she says. A few years after Michelle's death, though, he virtually moved into his beloved daughter's bedroom. "He spends a lot of time in there, but he won't talk about it," Vanessa says. "It's still too painful for him."

Shaka Franklin lived in a big, stylish house in an upmarket Denver suburb. At age sixteen he was a typical middle-class child of the 1980s—sports-obsessed, devoted to video games, computers, and rap music, blithe about school but a good student. A handsome kid, Shaka was more than six feet tall by his sixteenth birthday; he had also had to deal with his share of adult-sized challenges.

During his early teens his parents divorced, and since then his mother had been diagnosed with breast cancer, his father had developed diabetes, a grandmother to whom he'd been particularly close had died, and he was finding it difficult to adjust to his father's new girlfriend.

Shaka's father, Les Franklin, is a towering man—six feet five inches tall, with a solid build. By the end of the 1980s he had reached the top executive ranks at IBM in Colorado. Les continues to relive the final months of his son's life, trying to identify signs of Shaka's distress. For a long time, the feelings of guilt and shame that coursed through Les following his son's death in 1990 were incapacitating. And then there was the anger. "I was very angry, especially when I found out that Colorado had one of the highest teen suicide rates in the country," Les said during an address to the black suicide survivors' conference in Atlanta in February 1999. (A 1998 report by the Colorado governor's office said that 692 suicides were reported in that state in 1996, or about 55 per month, and suicide was the second leading cause of death among children, teens, and young adults.) "I was angry about it because no one had talked about it. . . . The parents didn't know, the school systems didn't seem to do anything. So I was bound and determined to go on a crusade to make people aware of the problem. . . . I was incredibly angry at the system."

During the early 1990s, Les began to channel the sadness and frustration he felt following his son's death into the founding of a nonprofit suicide awareness and prevention program.

His own story continues to evolve, and he constantly searches his conscience about his possible role in his son's death. But Les has also directed his energy and despair into a positive tribute to his son with activities that have begun to have a healthy impact on the lives of youth in Colorado. The Shaka Franklin Foundation for Youth is a community-based Denver group that offers tutoring, job training, and counseling to youngsters and their families. Its goal, along with offering constructive pursuits for young people in Denver, is to raise awareness among the region's political and business leaders about teens and mental health issues. For Les the early going was tough, yet he kept in his mind the belief that no other parent or child should ever have to go through what he'd experienced with his son. His inability to recognize the depths of Shaka's unhappiness still haunts him: "I saw my son's depression, but I didn't understand depression. I saw that he was down, but I just thought he was moody."

On October 19, 1990, Les reached the end of his workday with relief—a series of meetings had him feeling wound up, and he was glad to be heading home. He was well known in Denver, a high-level executive of a corporation that had a strong presence in the city's social and business arenas. Les's persistence and dedication to his job over the previous twenty years had afforded him a plush lifestyle—he lived in a "dream house," a showplace with an indoor swimming pool and thousands of square feet packed with all the amenities of late-twentieth-century affluence.

Les's family wanted for nothing in the way of material items, and he saw bright futures ahead for Shaka and his eldest son, Jamon. On that chilly autumn evening, he climbed into his black Porsche and set out for Gun Club Green, the exclusive subdivision where he lived with his sons and his girlfriend, who is now his wife. His divorce from the boys' mother a few years earlier had been tough on Shaka, but Les believed that both his sons had adjusted to it. Shaka hadn't warmed to Les's new romantic partner, Marianne, who had moved into their home, but he had never said outright that he blamed her or his father for the divorce. All the same, during the late 1980s Shaka's brother had noticed a change in him, an emotional distance that Jamon couldn't quite pinpoint. For Les, though, Shaka put on a "game face" —he was usually upbeat and had even begun showing hints of his father's strong will and calm intelligence. And certainly his physical appearance reflected that of his father.

That evening Les pulled his sparkling car into their wide garage, looking forward to greeting his youngest son; unless there was football practice at Thomas Jefferson High or some other school-related activity, Shaka would typically emerge from his room to meet his father with a slow smile and sometimes a bear hug.

But when Les called out for his son on that October night he was met by silence. After climbing the stairs of their split-level home, Les went to the door of Shaka's room and pushed it open.

He expected to find his son listening to hip-hop music or busy at the computer, two pastimes that he knew Shaka enjoyed immensely. Instead, Shaka lay on the floor of his bedroom, a wide red stain encircling his head. Then

Les saw the black revolver near his son's legs and he knew that Shaka would never again greet him with a shy hug and the words "How's it going, Pops?"

"There was a pain, an intense pain," recalls Les, who was fifty-one when Shaka killed himself. "It was so incredible, so overwhelming—I couldn't reason." Shaka had apparently gone into his father's closet and retrieved the snub-nosed .38 caliber Smith & Wesson revolver that Les kept hidden there. No suicide note was discovered, but a piece of heart-shaped wood that Shaka had carved some weeks earlier was found near his body. Written across it in purple ink were the words "Love, Shaka."

Late that night—after the authorities had come with their questions and procedures—Les walked out of the front door of his huge home and into a massive early-season snowstorm. Scantily clad, he raged around the neighborhood and along the surrounding roads for hours, cursing, crying, and yelling uncontrollably. "Here I am, this very large black man, wearing only [pants and] a T-shirt in freezing temperatures, running up and down the highways and screaming my lungs out—people looked at me like I was crazy. And at that time I was." Over the next month, close friends arrived from across the nation. "They kept me alive," Les says. "The guilt is what I felt foremost—I rehashed everything that had ever happened with my son, everything I'd ever said to him."

Over and over again Les remembered one incident in particular that had occurred just a few days before Shaka's death. "We were in the family room, watching a documentary, some program on suicide, and I said, 'Man, those folks are crazy!' Shaka just sat looking at the television screen—he never said a word." Later Les learned that Shaka had given away to friends some of his most treasured possessions in the days before his suicide—cassette tapes, CDs, a watch, even some of his favorite clothes.

Looking back, Les also recalls that a few weeks earlier he had told his youngest son that his former wife, Cherllyn, who lived in Connecticut, had had a recurrence of breast cancer and the prognosis was bleak. In hindsight Les realized that Shaka's response to an update about his mother's illness had seemed odd.

"When I told him that his mother was dying of cancer, he just tensed up. We didn't really talk about it." Indeed, during the breakup of their marriage and after, Les had assiduously avoided discussing his first wife with Shaka. "He wore his feelings on his sleeve," Les recalls. "But whenever he'd mention his mother, I didn't want to hear it—I shut down on his feelings about his mother and about our divorce. . . . Anything he had to say about his mom, I didn't want to hear. Looking back, now I know that he was angry about that." (Cherllyn died a few months after her son's suicide).

In the early days, Les also coped with his initial feelings by virtually shutting down. "I would go into the shower and scream at the top of my lungs, but I didn't want to discuss it with anyone."

Eventually, with the help of Jamon and of Marianne, who had become his wife, Les began to redirect his frustration at losing Shaka. "It was hard. I mean, I had to get through it all, the guilt, the shame, the embarrassment. I was a high-profile person in Denver, and my son's suicide had basically told everyone that things weren't so good in my household."

He went through periods of blaming himself–or the system, or other family members–for Shaka's death. Now, however, Les is part of a growing grassroots movement emerging in many American communities, one that hopes to prevent other teens from self-destructing. For black Americans especially, Les believes, there is much more to be done where mental health, suicide, and the public's perceptions about both are concerned.

"I think that for many African-Americans, for so long, part of the reason why suicide wasn't an issue is that we were working so hard just to keep ends together, to get a meal and keep our houses together, that we didn't have time to think about being depressed," Les told the black suicide survivors' group in Atlanta. Moreover, he continued, "We won't go to white psychologists or psychiatrists, and many blacks don't have access to mental health professionals who are African-American. And black men, especially, don't go to reach out to anybody when they are under stress. And unfortunately, that has been devastating to our community."

A few years after Shaka's death Les formed the foundation that bears his son's name. Shaka Franklin's story has appeared in a handful of black-interest magazines, and Les speaks to suicide prevention and mental health awareness groups around the nation if called upon.

He can reel off many disturbing statistics–for example, an average of more than 30,000 suicides were committed in the United States annually during the late 1990s, of which approximately 5,000 were teenagers; approximately 400,000 teens attempt suicide each year; and 5 or 6 black males committed suicide in Denver each year during the late 1990s. Les has become well versed in the terminology of depression and mental illness and the symptoms that might indicate an individual's suicidal thinking,[4] and he is convinced that a combined effort by parents, health care workers, and public officials may someday begin to reduce the incidence of suicide and other self-destructive behaviors.

"We've got to be able to talk about these issues," Les says. On March 5, 1998, when Colorado governor Roy Romer released a comprehensive suicide prevention and intervention plan,[5] a summary of Shaka's story, accompanied by a photo of him looking confident and relaxed in his school football uniform, was prominently displayed in the section titled "Risk Factors and Predictors of Suicide." For Les, staying involved in raising public awareness about suicide gives him a way of honoring his son—and a way of paying back some inexplicable debt that he feels he carries.

"Working with the foundation and with other groups on preventing suicide helps keep me alive," Les says bluntly. His avocation gained a new sense of urgency in the spring of 1999: one year after the Colorado governor's report on suicide prevention was released, two white male teenagers carried rifles and homemade bombs into a high school outside Denver and killed twelve students and teachers before turning their guns on themselves.

The full-color images were jarring, but they offered some consolation to Carla Johnson. On a hot summer morning in 1993, she showed a visitor half a dozen photographs of her youngest daughter, Jackie. The image of Carla's daughter was captured sharply on the postcard-sized pictures, her eyes closed, her hands folded neatly across her tiny chest. She wore a frilly white dress, its flounces indistinguishable from the snowy lining of the open coffin in which she lay: the photos had been taken by one of Carla's relatives at Jackie's wake. The visitation service took place at a mortuary on the poor side of Hollywood, Florida, a few days after Jackie, who was only six years old, stepped in front of a moving freight train. Two of the child's older siblings had been with her that morning, and they later told their mother and law enforcement officials that Jackie had deliberately stepped onto the tracks.

For Carla, her youngest daughter's death was the latest of several hard blows she had endured since the mid-1980s—abusive relationships with men, minor brushes with the law, and long stretches of unemployment relieved only by the help of relatives and public assistance. Then, in the early 1990s, Carla had learned that she had HIV, the virus that leads to AIDS. On the day she showed the photos of Jackie to this particular visitor, a month after her daughter's suicide, Carla was living in a small, hot room at her aunt's home and suffering from a powerful case of thrush–a fungus infection to which AIDS patients are particularly susceptible–which made her tongue swell to twice its normal size.

"I miss my baby so much," Carla said thickly. "I cry for her every day." It tore her up, wondering if she could have done something to prevent her youngest daughter's suicide: "If I had been able to talk to her, to try and find out what was going on, maybe it wouldn't have happened." Even though the virus had obliterated her immune system, making her susceptible to any little bug that happened along, Carla said she didn't believe that she would ever die from AIDS. And certainly, during that stifling early summer, she was facing mortality in a way that was much more immediate and tangible.

On June 15, 1993, the death of Jackie Johnson, a kindergartner in Broward County, shocked thousands of Floridians. Her story seemed simple, if unaccountably tragic–a little girl, distraught over her mother's illness but unable to talk about it with any adults, had ended her own life by standing in front of an oncoming train.

Jackie's death struck a chord with many people, black and white, rich and poor, because it seemed so fundamentally heartbreaking, so hopelessly sad that a child so young had made such an adult decision. Indeed, there was more to the short life and dramatic death of Jackie Johnson. To many in South Florida's overburdened community of social service workers, Jackie's death was tied to the plight of thousands of black and Latino women who were struggling with the AIDS virus fifteen years after the disease first surfaced in America. The same stigma, shame, and fear of ridicule that kept–and continues to keep–millions of black and brown people from coming forward with their HIV diagnoses, and from taking control over their sexual well-being, played a part in Jackie's fatal act.

Jackie's mother had feared "coming out" about her illness. To Carla, the decision not to discuss her HIV status with her children had seemed wise at the time she'd made it. But after Jackie's suicide and the attention it received in the local news media, Carla feared that her four surviving children would have to bear a double stigma, that their peers would taunt them because their sister had killed herself and because their mother was dying from an illness that some believed was a blight from God. Crying softly, Carla said she feared for her children's future. She had tried to protect them by not telling them about her illness, but they had found out anyway. And, Carla said, she hoped to see Jackie again someday—in heaven.

Several months earlier, on Easter morning 1993, Carla had awoken to find that she couldn't walk. She had been diagnosed with HIV in 1992, almost a year before, and had known she was HIV positive when she gave birth to her youngest son, a boy who was now a year old. She had been treated at a local public hospital, whose doctors had prescribed a medication schedule, but she didn't always have the money for the daunting array of pills. And since she never seemed to have anything worse than an occasional flu-like illness, taking the medicine every day was not always her top priority. Before the HIV diagnosis, she recalled, "I was always healthy. I hardly ever had colds or anything."

Carla's life had been relatively uneventful. She grew up in a small town in south Broward County called Dania, a predominantly black inland community miles removed from the expensive homes, condominiums, and resorts that line the white-sand beaches along the Atlantic Ocean. She gave birth to her first child, a boy named Velarius, while she was in her early twenties, and had four more children by 1993, including Jackie. She had graduated from high school in the early 1980s and worked odd jobs for the next few years—monotonous gigs, mostly. One job she'd held was at a local bottling company, another at a pencil manufacturer, and there were also occasional stints as a maid in one of the hotels by the beach in Fort Lauderdale. Her best friend in 1993 was a woman she'd gone to middle school with. Carla said she gave up "going out" when she started having children. For more than ten years she received public assistance.

Her large extended family—her aunts, cousins, uncles, and two siblings—were always willing to help support her and her children, she said, even though they all sometimes struggled to make ends meet in their own households. Carla's father, E. L. Johnson, died in 1991, when a blood vessel burst in his brain. "I miss him a lot," Carla said. She had never felt close to her mother and spent much of her young adult life in the home of Laura Scott, the aunt who took her in a few months before Jackie's suicide. Carla had, a few days before her daughter's death, completed legal papers granting custody of her children to Laura Scott. She viewed her aunt Laura as a person of integrity and reliability, and suspected that some of her other relatives might want to claim her children in order to collect foster-care money.

Paradoxically, Carla had been preparing for the eventuality of her own death even as she denied that she believed she would die of AIDS. And she was loath to have the community know the extent–or the origin–of her illness. Carla said that she knew many blacks who viewed AIDS as a disease one "caught" from having anal sex or shooting drugs. Until Jackie died, Carla had resisted talking with anyone but her social worker about her HIV status. In the aftermath of Jackie's suicide, she was shocked at some of the speculation that had appeared in local news reports: one Miami-based television news program had reported, without attributing the information to Carla or any authorized surrogate, that "the mother of the girl who killed herself is suffering from AIDS."

In Carla's mind, the news report was irresponsible and incorrect. "I may have been diagnosed with HIV, but I do not have AIDS," she maintained. She had declined to talk with reporters in the days immediately following her daughter's death, and had forbade her social worker and the caregivers at the hospital where she had been treated from talking to the press. But a month after Jackie's suicide, after the frenzy of interest from South Florida's ravenous television news teams had abated, Carla agreed to be interviewed by coauthor Amy Alexander for the *Miami Herald*. She met with Alexander, in part, to clear up what she saw as misinformation that had been reported about her illness and about the details of her daughter's death.

Despite the thrush, which had caused her to be hospitalized in the weeks before Jackie's death, Carla said she believed she would somehow escape developing full-blown AIDS. The cousin of one of her best friends had the disease, and Carla had gone to the hospital several months before to visit the woman. "She was all hooked up to breathing machines and everything . . . It was horrible," Carla said. "I said to myself when I saw her, 'I don't ever want to be like that.'" And, again, Carla reiterated her denial that she would actually die from AIDS. "I gathered up the kids last night and told them how much I love them," she said. "I told them not to believe what they've been hearing . . . 'Mama is not going to die,' I told them."

Exactly how Carla Johnson may have contracted HIV, and how her health status might have been connected to her daughter's suicide, was the focus of inquiries by Amy Alexander and others.

For a few months during the late 1980s, Carla lived in Pompano Beach, a quiet city just north of Fort Lauderdale, with a boyfriend. She knew that the man had been an intravenous drug user, but he had "cleaned up" by the time she moved in with him. "All of a sudden, he got real sick," Carla said. "I mean, one minute he had a cold, and then it just got worse and worse." Carla did not disclose his name, but she said that he never "owned up" to having AIDS. She left him and didn't know what had become of him.

Carla said she might have contracted the virus from another man, a former boyfriend who is the father of her two youngest children. This man had been in prison before Carla began her relationship with him. After she had been with him for a few months, she learned that he had had a homosexual experience during his time in prison. When Carla confronted him about it he got angry. "Every time I'd try and bring it up, we'd get in a fist fight," she said. Carla ruled out the fathers of two of her other children, saying that neither of those men had drug abuse or jail in their histories. Her youngest son, the child who was a year old when Jackie committed suicide, showed signs of the antibodies that might indicate the presence of HIV. But as the boy grew, the HIV antibodies transferred to him from Carla while in utero slowly disappeared and several months later additional testing had shown that he was not HIV positive.

Sometime in early June of 1993, a relative of Carla's, an aunt with a drinking problem who always seemed to be in trouble, told Carla's children that their mother had AIDS. Later, when Carla realized that her children knew what had caused her to develop the painful thrush infection, she was furious: "[She] shouldn't have done that. If I had known that they knew, I would have talked to them about it." She entered Memorial Hospital in Hollywood, Florida, on May 25, 1993, and remained there for three weeks. Eating had become almost impossible and Carla had dropped more than fifteen pounds from her already slim frame. While at Memorial, she rested and tried to calmly consider her future. "They gave me a blood transfusion, some vitamins, and other medicine" is how she described her treatment there.

Over the years, Carla had developed a strong disdain for hospitals and clinics; she had marched out of waiting rooms after being treated rudely by workers or idling for hours awaiting treatment. Her social worker, a quiet-spoken young black woman named Marie Brown, had been involved with Carla's case since 1992. Unfortunately, according to Brown, Carla's unhappy experiences with the medical system were all too typical of what many poor single women of color go through. "We went to a community health center recently, and I can see why Carla gets frustrated by the medical system," Brown told Amy Alexander in an interview that took place a few days after Carla's talk with Alexander for the *Miami Herald* story.

During the clinic visit that Brown attended, Carla waited for several hours in a dingy reception area, and then, when her name was finally called, the doctor, who was white, was extremely curt. Brown recalled, "He looked at her and said, 'Oh I remember you–you're the one in denial. . . . I couldn't believe he'd said it, but he did." She knew that Carla had yet to come to terms with the implications of her HIV diagnosis, but Marie Brown had taken a patient and gradual tack in educating her client about the disease.

On June 3, 1993, Brown brought Carla's oldest children, including Jackie, to Memorial Hospital to visit their mother. According to Carla, Jackie didn't seem depressed during the visit, but she did notice that at one point Jackie had a "strange look" on her face: "She just said she loved me and that she wanted me to come home."

Shortly after 8 A.M. on June 15, a kindergarten teacher at Dania Elementary School, a no-nonsense woman named Winsome Bright, had just finished some paperwork. Her classroom aide, a young teaching student, was leading the pupils in a daily exercise they called "sharing time." Bright was half-listening as a young boy stood at his desk and began his turn to share some news. "He stood up and said that Jackie had been hit by a train," she reported several weeks later.

In a flash, Bright left the classroom and ran to the school's front office, where she learned that it was true. One of her students, a quiet, thoughtful girl named Jackie, had been killed that morning: "The hospital had just called the school. . . . We were shocked."

Carla had met the teacher only once during her daughter's time at Dania Elementary. "I had been sending Carla notes for parent-teacher conferences for some time, and one afternoon she just showed up," Bright said. "She was nice, and seemed real interested in how Jackie was doing in class. None of the staff at the school knew she was sick." Indeed, both Winsome Bright and Marie Brown remarked that they thought Carla was "a great mother."

Carla was resting at her aunt's house on the morning Jackie died; she had been released from Memorial Hospital a few days earlier. As she lay on the couch in Laura's small living room, another relative came bursting in. "My cousin came in and said that Jackie had been hit by a train," Carla said. "I started crying." Within minutes, Carla and other relatives rushed to the path her children walked on the way to school each morning, to the part of the route that took the kids near the railroad tracks.

As she arrived, Carla saw a phalanx of emergency service vehicles and a clutch of television news station vans. Her daughter was on a gurney at the rear doors of one of the ambulances, being lifted inside by two large paramedics. "They wouldn't let me near her," Carla said, so she and a relative followed the ambulance to Memorial Hospital in their car.

Later her oldest son and daughter—Velarius, who was eight, and Stephiteria, seven—told Carla that as they walked to school that morning along the tracks Jackie had told them that she wanted to get hit by the train; she had insisted, the children told Carla, that she wanted to "be with the angels" when her mother arrived in heaven. The little girl had run onto the tracks, the children said, and as the engine loomed, she turned her back toward the oncoming train. The engine's cowcatcher clipped the back of Jackie's legs and sent her flying: she landed some twenty feet away, the back of her head crushed and her neck broken. From the front, the children told Carla, she looked like she was sleeping.

At Memorial Hospital, Carla, her two older children, and other relatives waited while doctors worked on Jackie. "Then they came out and told us," Carla recalled, her voice trailing away. She had never thought of Jackie—whom she described as a strong-willed tomboy—as being particularly religious. But they had belonged to a Baptist church in Hollywood, and Jackie had always said that she enjoyed going to Sunday school and the day-long services.

Sometimes Carla or Aunt Laura would take Jackie to Wednesday evening services, when the choir sang long into the night and the minister shouted and testified about the glory of God and the righteousness of heaven. The children who were with Jackie when she died told Carla that the little girl had twisted away from them when they tried to drag her off of the tracks, saying again and again that she wanted to "be with the angels." And Velarius later told his mother that Jackie had talked of walking in front of the train several times before. "We knew she was serious when she did it," he said during an interview a month after his sister's death.

On the day after Jackie Johnson died Carla was readmitted to Memorial Hospital. The stress caused by her daughter's suicide may have exacerbated her condition, for she couldn't keep food down. She ventured out to sit in the front pew at Jackie's funeral, crying steadily as the minister eulogized her little girl; not once did the pastor mention AIDS or HIV. Then Carla went back to the hospital for several weeks before returning to her aunt's home, where she began spending most of her time in her small bedroom, agoniz-ing over what might have been: if only she had been aware that her children knew the nature of her illness back in early June, when they had visited her at Memorial.

"She wanted to be with me and the angels," Carla said, her red-rimmed eyes again scanning the snapshots of her daughter's body. "And now she's with my daddy." Thirteen months after Jackie's suicide, Carla Johnson died from complications of AIDS.

There is little research on suicide among children as young as Jackie Johnson. For the period from 1994 to 1997, the Centers for Disease Control report no suicide deaths among children under five years old, and an aver-age of about 5 deaths per year for children between five and nine years of age. However, the number of suicides rises to over 300 per year for children aged ten to fourteen, and for teenagers between fifteen and nineteen there is a dramatic six-fold jump, to over 1,800 suicides per year.[6]

Youth suicide studies have consistently shown that young people who kill themselves–particularly adolescents–are likely experiencing risk fac-tors that are familiar to mental health experts, including depression and stress. They may also, however, experience risk factors that might be harder to recognize, including ideas and fantasies about what it means to die. In-deed, as the case of Jackie Johnson illustrates, young children who express suicidal thoughts or who engage in suicidal behavior may believe that they do not really die if they kill themselves. "They may think something won-derful is going to happen," said Jon A. Shaw, director of child-adolescent psychiatry at the University of Miami, following Jackie's death in 1993. "Some fantasize that if they die, mom and dad will get back together or there will be a reunion with a dead parent."

Additionally, genetic or biological disorders in some children may make them more susceptible to depression and, subsequently, to self-destructive behaviors. Ultimately, mental health care providers and educators must be vigilant to signs of psychological or emotional stress in young children, no matter how trivial they may appear at first glance.

The examples of Michelle Jackson, Shaka Franklin, and Jackie Johnson provide but a shapshot of the multitude of elements that combine to create environments that foster suicide among black Americans. Additionally, in the late 1990s the complicated array of elements which have been recognized as part of the suicide equation—despair, mental illness, a sense of hopelessness, drug and alcohol abuse—were joined by a postmodern collection of highly volatile risk factors, including the increasing availability of firearms, the rising rate of incarceration for black men, and the presence of AIDS.

Mental illness, such as the depression that Michelle Jackson experienced, is perhaps the most treatable of the physiological risk factors that contribute to suicide or self-destructive behavior in blacks, and in the general population. One of the largest challenges facing public policy experts and public health officials, however, stems from the political and economic difficulties that inevitably accompany any effort to address the organic and societal influences that contribute to an individual's potential for suicide. Funding initiatives that could make it possible for troubled people to find early treatment for drug and alcohol abuse and mental illness are not politically popular. Furthermore, the historic reluctance among health officials to link suicide to mental illness has severely limited the public's understanding of its connection with psychological risk factors like depression.

Of course the social and cultural influences which contribute to a suicide-friendly environment, as well as the long-term negative impact of racism and poverty, are formidable obstacles to the search for solutions to the problem of the growing numbers of blacks who kill themselves. The legacies of American history, including the troubled relationship between blacks and the medical community, must also be considered in any attempt to neutralize some of the cultural and social elements that may contribute to suicidal and self-destructive behaviors. We will discuss these factors at length in the following chapters.

2

Suicide in Black and White

Theories and Statistics

T he enigma of suicide has fascinated and frustrated humankind for centuries. No one in the long history of Western culture has solved its riddle, though generations of philosophers, theologians, and psychoanalysts
have tried. As a subject of psychological study, it has inspired volumes of literature–theories, statistical studies, and professional journal articles. But
in American society at large, it is safe to say, suicide is rarely a welcome topic
of public discourse: for survivors in particular, any discussion of why people kill themselves is sad and frightening, a slippery road that is invariably
marked by the twists and turns of shame, guilt, and seemingly unanswer-
able questions. The less said about suicide publicly, the better, has long been
the attitude of most citizens, especially African-Americans. Suicide, in the
perception of many, is anathema to the American doctrine of being strong
in the face of adversity, of forging ahead and seizing the day.

As we touched upon in the preceding chapter, among black Americans
the reticence to confront suicide and self-destructive behavior has been
shaped by key historic and cultural elements, including slavery, racism,
poverty, and discrimination. Distinct from the experience of most white
Americans, these cultural elements encourage many blacks to will away
perceived weaknesses, such as suicidal thoughts, in the name of self-
preservation and dignity. In addition, the Christian religious beliefs of

many blacks hold that suicide is taboo, a sin that will prevent one's soul from gaining entrance to heaven.

Historically, several differences in the dynamics of suicide among blacks and whites have been noted by public health officials: blacks have been less disposed to suicide than whites; white men have had higher suicide rates than black men, and both these groups have had higher suicide rates than black women; elderly white men are more likely to kill themselves than elderly black men or women. These and other historical and clinical facts about suicide are largely unknown to the layperson, however, and until recently there has been little public incentive to do other than look away from what is admittedly an unsettling subject. In the late 1990s, though, signs emerged that Americans would ultimately have to come to terms with suicide as a public health issue for all, and especially for African-Americans.

In 1999, the Surgeon General of the United States, Dr. David Satcher, announced that suicide had become the ninth leading cause of death for all Americans, and the third leading cause of death for those between the ages of fifteen and twenty-four. And while the rate of serious crime in the country had dropped, an average of 85 suicides were taking place each day. As a cause of death in the United States, as a public health problem, the total number of suicides had, by the late 1990s, topped that of homicides, at about 31,000 deaths per year compared with about 21,000 homicides.

While it is important to note that during the twenty-year period between the 1970s and 1999 the total suicide rate in America declined, from 12.1 deaths per 100,000 in 1976 to 10.8 in 1996, the suicide rate among teenagers and young adults nearly tripled during that same period.[1] Meanwhile, according to the United States Centers for Disease Control (CDC), the rate of suicides among black males climbed from 7.9 per 100,000 persons in 1970 to 10.9 per 100,000 in 1997, with the suicide rate for all blacks also increasing, although less rapidly, during the same period, from 5.1 in 1970 to 6.1 in 1997.[2]

Black women, on the other hand, have experienced low rates of suicide in all age groups, when compared with whites or with black men. In 1970, for example, the rate of suicide among white women was 7.1 per 100,000, as compared to 2.6 for black women; by 1995, the rate for white women was 4.4, versus 2.0 for black women; for black men in 1970 the suicide rate was 7.9, and in 1995 it was 12.4, compared to 19.7 for white men.[3]

The social dynamics behind these figures are worth examining. The rising rate of suicide among black men, in contrast to black women and especially compared with the comparatively modest increase in the total suicide rate, leads to many questions: What are the different risk factors effecting black men and black women? How do black men respond to stress? How do black women respond to stress? What role does the national economy and the availability of employment play in the disparity in suicide rates between black men and women, and between blacks and whites? Did the nation's cultural and political tone during the twenty-year window of 1979 to 1999 have any impact on the suicide rates of blacks or whites? What about violence in the media? Is the availability of guns a part of the equation? What coping mechanisms, or lack thereof, effect suicide rates among the different age, sex, income, and racial groups?

The gap between black suicide rates and white rates has begun to shrink, with black rates climbing to unparalleled and alarming heights. To be sure, there seem to be similarities in the elements driving the increase in black suicides and the increase in suicide in America's total youth population. We know that depression and isolation are two primary psychological risk factors that are likely precursors to suicidal ideation in individuals. (The suicide rate among Native Americans, arguably the most isolated ethnic group in the country, was 1.5 times that of the total U.S. population between 1979 and 1992, according to the CDC.)[4] And by the end of the 1990s, a sense of hopelessness and isolation could be perceived below the surface of American culture at large–a kind of equal-opportunity millenial malaise that crossed ethnic lines despite the healthy economic gains seen by millions of Americans as the century drew to a close. But where a modest decline in the homicide rate in the United States drew much political and media attention during the late 1990s, the increase in suicides among the young, and the factors which distinguish suicide in different ethnic populations, were scarcely acknowledged by the body politic.

Then a series of high profile murder-suicides occurred during an eighteen-month period between 1997 and 1999 (murder-suicides account for 1.5 to 4 percent of all suicides).[5] These killings included several instances where white males gunned down family members, friends, coworkers, strangers, or classmates before killing themselves. This brought the uncomfortable subjects of suicide, mental health, racism, violence, and the availability of guns into the nation's living rooms. A kind of free-floating despair was leading white males to commit a form of violence that wasn't supposed to happen in suburban America.

Many African-Americans, however, are intimately familiar with the connection between homicide and suicide, with violent behavior that springs outward before turning in on itself. Although they account for only about 13 percent of the total population, blacks, primarily males, account for about half of all deaths by homicide in the United States. Couldn't these killings have been precipitated by individuals suffering from a lack of self-worth and other emotional dynamics that are similar to suicidal behaviors? Few public discussions made such a link. Nonetheless, the surgeon general's announcement in July 1999 that suicide had become a public health issue appeared timely, coming at a moment when America had in its sights vivid images of suicide.

For all the official presence and credibility of his office, Surgeon General David Satcher faced a monumentally difficult triple task. How to simultaneously address the complicated causal factors of suicide and risky behavior in modern America and launch an effective campaign to educate the citizenry about the clinical and scientific facts while strengthening prevention programs for suicide and its cousins, homicide and substance abuse? There were no answers at the ready because there has been so little conclusive research on the subject. At the same time, the historic and religious view of suicide as shameful predominated.

Throughout the history of the civilized world, this was not always the case, even in the West. In some cultures, instances of self-destruction were tolerated by custom or religious philosophy, or accepted as an alternative to shame or death at the hands of others. In ancient Greece, of course, Socrates accepted a cup of hemlock. In Shakespeare's great tragedy *Hamlet* the protagonist utters the famous words "To be or not to be," effectively capturing the ambiguity of suicide; considering his secular and spiritual dilemma, the Dane asks himself if it would be "nobler" to suffer "life's slings and arrows," or "to take arms against a sea of troubles, and by opposing end them."

Viewed in other cultural and historic contexts worldwide, not all instances of self-murder were considered signs of "sickness." In ancient Japan, an aristocrat or a warrior might commit culturally sanctioned ritual suicide—one form of which was *hara-kiri*—rather than face dishonor or capture by enemies. (The connection between the way suicide was perceived earlier in Japanese history and its current status is not entirely clear, although by the late 1990s the suicide rate in Japan—where little shameful stigma is attached—had climbed to 19.3 per 100,000 individuals, a figure that officials attribute in part to hopelessness and despair among middle-aged Japanese men struggling to keep afloat in a tough economy.)[6] In India, following the ancient Hindu custom of *suttee*, some women sacrificed themselves on their husbands' funeral pyres as proof of their love and devotion. (*Suttee* was prohibited by the British in the nineteenth century but persisted for a time in isolated orthodox communities.)

While early Christians often embraced martyrdom as evidence of their faith, Christianity, Judaism, and Islam have regarded suicide as a crime against nature and God: life is sacred and what God gives, only God can take away. Some branches of these religions deny burial in consecrated ground to people who kill themselves, unless the suicide is deemed unintentional. In feudal England, suicide was considered a criminal act because a person who killed himself or herself had broken his or her bond of fealty to the Crown; in some American states, attempted suicide was long considered an indictable offense.

Over the centuries, sociologists, psychologists, and psychiatrists in the West have scrutinized suicide to determine its causes and forestall its occurrence. Emile Durkheim, in his groundbreaking work *Suicide*, first published in 1897,[7] applied the word to "all cases of death resulting directly or indirectly from a positive or negative act of the victim himself, which he knows will produce this result." Durkheim divided suicide into three major types—egoistic, altruistic, and anomic.

Egoistic suicide results from the individual's failure to fit into his society; as Durkheim explained it (following the convention of his day, in which "the individual" was always "he"), the individual with weak community, religious, family, political, and social ties destroys himself because he can find no basis for existing. Altruistic suicide results from the domination of the individual by a group, wherein the group's authority becomes so complete that the individual loses his sense of personal identity and sacrifices his life for the collective body. (The murder-suicides of 914 members of the People's Temple in Guyana in 1978 appear to fit this model, as do the 1997 suicides of more than 20 members of the Heaven's Gate cult in San Diego.) Other examples of altruistic suicide might include a soldier who dies "for his country" or a Buddhist priest who immolates himself to protest a war.

Anomic suicide results from anomie–a state of alienation and lack of purpose due to the individual's failure to adjust to social change, including severe economic reverses or other events leading to social dislocation.

And, according to Durkheim, "There is [another] type of suicide that is the opposite of anomic suicide. . . . It is the suicide deriving from excessive regulation, that of persons with futures pitilessly blocked and passions violently choked by oppressive discipline." Durkheim did not consider this fourth type of suicide, which he termed fatalistic suicide, significant. It is this concept, however, that we believe is most important if one is to begin understanding suicide among blacks.

Although Durkheim cited few examples of fatalistic suicide, he believed it might be of historical interest: "Do not the suicides of slaves . . . belong to this type, or all suicides attributable to excessive physical or moral despotism? [It is the revolt against] the ineluctable and inflexible nature of a rule against which there is no appeal."

David Lester, author of numerous books and papers on suicide, including *Suicide in African-Americans* (1998),[8] found that "suicide was very common among . . . slaves when they were captured, while they were being transported to America, and immediately upon arrival." Writing in the spring 1997 issue of *Suicide and Life-Threatening Behavior,* the journal of the American Association of Suicidology, Lester found evidence that, while fragmented, indicated that these suicides among Africans bound for colonial America occurred in part because of rumors widespread in Africa that "Whites cooked and ate the captured Africans," and because "slaves watching Whites drink red wine often thought they were drinking blood."[9] Lester and a handful of other suicidologists have produced spare but meaningful historic evidence indicating that since at least the seventeenth century some blacks chose to end their own lives rather than endure slavery.

Over the years, the formation of theories on blacks and suicide by (mostly white) clinical professionals has been spotty and unreliable, and any citations of exact numbers of black suicides before the early twentieth century are based on shoddy record-keeping and/or speculative projections. Furthermore, the world community of psychotherapists formed its general ideas about suicide without much consideration of the experiences of blacks and other enslaved or oppressed groups. Nevertheless, a review of the literature by pioneer theorists and researchers provides key insights for our consideration of suicide and self-destructive behavior among U.S. blacks today.

Sigmund Freud, Durkheim's contemporary, proposed in "Mourning and Melancholia," a 1917 paper,[10] that suicide is aggression against others turned upon oneself. He theorized that self-hatred as manifested in depression is a result of repressed rage toward a love object or an oppressor (a hated object) and turned back on the self. We believe that this theoretical formulation is very relevant in thinking about the dynamics of black suicide. Freud also suggested that, unconsciously, many people who decide to commit suicide believe they will not really die–a phenomenom most common among teenagers and young adults–and that they will somehow be able to reverse the action if they so choose. In 1938, a study by researcher Gregory Zilboorg demonstrated the significance of repressed fantasies of immortality, particularly in suicidal patients.[11]

Alfred Adler, for a time a colleague of Freud, suggested that by an act of self-destruction the individual hopes to evoke sympathy for himself/herself and cast reproach upon those responsible for his/her lack of self-esteem.[12] Sandor Rado stressed the importance of dependency and atonement in depression; like Freud, he believed that suicide is an expression of "retroflexed anger," but he saw its goal as being self-punishment in an attempt to retrieve the affection or attention of a lost love interest.[13] This concept is also important when considering black suicides, particularly among young black males, for whom notoriety and the notion of "being somebody" might lead to either suicidal or homicidal behavior.

In 1957, researchers Edwin Schneidman and Norman Farberow divided suicidal persons into four general classes: those who view suicide as a honorable act, as a transition to a better life, or as a means of avoiding social disgrace; those who are bereaved or in ill health and physical pain and view suicide as an escape from deep anguish; those who are suffering from psychosis and kill themselves in response to hallucinations or delusions; and, finally, those who commit suicide out of spite and anger in the hope that the people whom they are trying to punish will suffer.[14] According to Schneidman and Farberow, serious losses (or threats of loss)–of friends, family, money, status, pride, independence, or social power–have the greatest causal significance. In 1984, researchers Moses Laufer and M. Egle Laufer theorized that every suicide attempt should be seen as a psychotic episode.[15]

In 1998, however, psychiatrist John T. Maltsberger posited that a key dynamic in suicidal patients was the projection of their own self-hatred onto the outside world, a projection that, in turn, makes the world seem to the depressed patient unfriendly and hostile, resulting in intolerable mental anguish.[16] (This dynamic can be applicable in homicidal behavior, as well.)

Finally, in addition to these important psychological explanations, in recent years researchers have been searching for neurological correlates of suicide. Thus far, none have arrived at definitive conclusions, but the research into the physiological and psychological elements of suicide continues.

Psychodynamic theories provide valuable insights into the causes of suicide, and, taken together, they imply that psychosocial and cultural factors may matter a great deal, particularly when considering black suicide. What can statistics tell us about these factors?

During much of American history, it has been difficult to determine the exact rate of suicide in society and in the black community. However, for most of the twentieth century, suicide was listed by the government as one of the ten leading causes of death in the United States. In 1933, during the Great Depression, the rate of suicidal deaths per 100,000 population, an annual figure which applies to all ages, races, and both sexes, reached an all-time high of 17.4. Although this rate declined during the 1940s and 1950s, suicide still remained among the top ten causes of death for all ages. Suicide rates began to climb again in the late 1960s, and by the late 1990s suicide became the third leading cause of death for those aged fifteen to twenty-four years old.[17]

The demographics and specifics behind the rise and fall of overall suicide rates are intriguing, and, popular beliefs aside, the available data does support some common threads. There are approximately ten unsuccessful suicide attempts for every fatal one. Suicide is most common among men, though women generally attempt it three times as often as men do. Self-destruction occurs least among children under fifteen and most among males over age sixty-five. In general, suicide rates are high among the lonely, the widowed, and the divorced. In the past, rates were highest in big cities and lowest in rural regions. More recent statistics, however, show that urban and rural suicide rates are equalizing.

Men have more often killed themselves by shooting or hanging, whereas women have tended to use passive methods such as the ingestion of poison or sleeping medication; although the cutting of wrists was also more likely to be chosen by women. Since the 1950s, though, firearms have increasingly become the chosen tool for committing suicide: the government reported that in 1997, the most recent year for which figures were available, guns were used in the majority of U.S. suicides, 17,566, compared with 13,522 gun-related homicides in that year.[18]

The economy of a given era, as we've seen with the high suicide rate during the Great Depression, also plays a role. But interestingly, during periods of stability doctors, dentists, and lawyers commit suicide three times more often than nonprofessional white-collar workers do. And it is important to emphasize that persons of any age, race, socioeconomic group, religion, or sex can be at risk for suicidal death when stressful conditions arise which the individual sees as being beyond their capability to manage.

Social scientists have been baffled by the fact that traditionally the rate of suicide among blacks—who were cast throughout history as America's hard-luck group—has been much lower than that of whites. Of course, the reporting of suicides both for the general population and for blacks has been unsophisticated for much of this century; even today, the nation's official keeper of suicide statistics, the CDC, must rely on annual figures collected by coroners and medical examiners in local jurisdictions. A lack of uniformity in reporting, and in the collection of control-group information like the income and education level of those who committed suicide, hobbles the government's ability to attain suicide figures that are reliably comprehensive.

It is difficult to identify all of the similarities and divergences in black and white suicide rates and place them in the context of cultural and social dynamics over the years. Nevertheless, in upcoming chapters we will examine the varieties of psychosocial, cultural, and socioeconomic factors which we believe provide the underpinnings for the rise in black suicide, particularly among black males aged fifteen to forty-four.

A dearth of encompassing research that takes into account possible regional influences on the suicide rates makes it difficult to assess the meanings of any differences between suicide rates in different parts of the country. Data from a 1998 CDC report, however, indicate that black suicide rates have historically been higher in the North and West than in the South, although that had changed by the end of the 1990s, when the suicide rate among black men in their twenties in the Deep South increased by more than 200 percent by 1997. In that same report, the CDC revealed that the overall rate of suicide in black communities in the Deep South appeared to be approaching that of blacks in the North and in the Midwest.[19] And, as we've noted, at least one nationwide trend has appeared: since the late 1970s, the rate of increase in suicides among black men in their twenties has been alarmingly steady. This development raises a salient question: Since the social condition of blacks and other minorities in the United States often serves as a bellwether to the condition of the white populace, is the increase in black male suicide an early warning sign of what lies ahead for the nation?

Most contemporary investigators agree that the disruption of social relations is a major cause of suicide. Undeniably, black men in America have experienced a greater degree of several forms of social dislocation than most other groups.

Psychiatrists E. Stanley and T. Barters, and child therapist F. V. Wenz found during the 1970s that adolescents lacking one parent were more likely to attempt suicide than those living with two parents.[20] This factor may well be of special significance in the black community, where by 1995 almost 60 percent of all black children lived in female-headed households and 45 percent of black female-headed households had incomes at or below the poverty level.[21] In terms of what they indicate about the social conditions which might lead to suicidal and self-destructive behavior, these statistics relate to other realities of life for many African-Americans.

Black mothers in single-parent households, struggling to keep kith and kin together, often meet with racial as well as gender-based discrimination in the job market, a development which obviously negatively effects the well-being of their families. Indeed, as noted above, for more than thirty years the majority of female-headed black households in America have shown incomes at or below the poverty level. Many of the women heading these households cannot find affordable child care or medical care, a situation which is dire enough to begin with and may lead to the abuse or neglect of their children. Although it is true that thousands of children from such households manage to grow into healthy and productive citizens, there are also many thousands who face gloomy futures as a result of their difficult beginnings. We also know from uncounted government and academic studies that children who are abused and neglected are at greater risk for exhibiting violent behavior, which increases the likelihood of homicide and suicide.[22]

Many black children from low-income, female-headed households drop out of school or are expelled at high rates; they also tend to lag behind in learning and are more likely than children from two-parent households to be labeled "educable mentally retarded," or "learning disabled." In addition, millions of black children attend schools that remain, despite the official end of segregation in the 1950s, racially and economically segregated, and many black children continue to experience direct forms of racial discrimination while in school. In counterpoint, some investigators have noted that the extraordinary commitment black women have demonstrated toward their children and for their homes helps these children withstand severe depression, and may account, in part for the comparatively low suicide rates of black women and youth during most of the twentieth century.

In his 1969 work *Suicide*, Jack P. Gibbs, suggested that the suicide rate depends on the general equilibrium of a given society: when there is turmoil and instability in a group, the suicide rate among group members rises; when individuals are planted securely in a community and there is little social change, the suicide rate decreases.[23] This theory has been used to account for the current rise in suicide among blacks. When blacks were uniformly segregated, poor, and firmly held "in their place," the reasoning goes, there was little disruption among them and thus a low suicide rate–but with greater freedom, increased mobility, and the breakdown of formal segregation as blacks moved from rural to urban settings, the incidence of suicide among them increased. (As we noted earlier, without supporting research from psychologists or psychiatrists, a March 1998 story in the *New York Times* detailing high suicide rates among young black males seized on a truncated modern version of this argument; the story, while accurately citing CDC figures showing an increase in black male suicides, speculated that young African-American adults were struggling with a "new affluence" and seemed to be choosing suicide as an escape from its unexpected stresses.)[24] As early as 1938, Charles Prudhomme, a black psychoanalyst, had predicted that the black suicide rate would approach the white rate as blacks assimilated.[25]

The implications of such theories are intriguing, problematic, and almost impossible to gauge. What does it say about black American character if the long overdue, hard-won middle-class status is finally achieved only to result in a stressful combination of self-doubt, racial fatigue, dissatisfaction, and confusion that leads to suicide? Since the CDC has only recently began collecting income and education-level information about black suicide victims, it is impossible–and inappropriate–to promulgate a theory in which black "middle-class angst" is driving the rise in black suicides.

In the second half of the twentieth century, some investigators, perhaps taking a cue from Durkheim, believed that the increase in the black suicide rate took place because of a sense of fatalism–a feeling of oppression and of being trapped by and within a society that does not allow one to realize one's aspirations. For example, the high unemployment rate among blacks during much of the twentieth century, particularly among young black males, is in fact the most critical index of the deleterious effect of economic factors on African-American health. In a 1977 paper, M. Harvey Brenner demonstrated a rise in admissions to mental hospitals during jumps in unemployment, and a decrease in admissions during times of relative economic prosperity. Looking at U.S. Census figures in 1970, Brenner calculated that a 1 percent increase in unemployment, representing nearly one million people, sustained for six years, would lead to the following:

- 36,887 total deaths, including 20,420 from heart disease
- 920 suicides
- 640 homicides
- 495 deaths from cirrhosis of the liver, which is often related to chronic alcoholism
- 4,277 state hospital admissions[26]

Brenner reported that every 1 percent rise in unemployment was accompanied by a 2 percent increase in the mortality rate, about a 2 percent increase in cardiovascular deaths, a 5 to 6 percent rise in homicides, a 5 percent increase in imprisonment, a 3 to 4 percent rise in first admissions to mental hospitals, and about a 5 percent increase in infant mortality. Under such conditions, the rate of suicide would also significantly increase.

With unemployment rates near 20 percent for all blacks, and about 45 percent for black youths during the twenty years between 1970 and the early 1990s, the impact on African-American health (particularly that of black males) has been dire. In 1998 the unemployment rate for blacks was 8.9 percent, lower than it had been in many years. According to the Bureau of Labor Statistics, in 1998 the unemployment rate for white males over age twenty reached a historic low of 3.2 percent. For black males aged sixteen to twenty-four years, though, the unemployment rate was 20.7 percent in 1998.[27] The high rate of black joblessness—even as millions of blacks entered the middle class during the 1980s and 1990s—pushed high numbers of African-Americans into the ranks of the poor. And while one's income is not always a predictor of one's mental or physical health, we know that individuals who cannot afford health care are more likely to experience serious illnesses.

Writing in *Minority Mental Health,* in 1982, researcher H. F. Myers observed,

> By nature, poverty is an illness-inducing state because of the excessive and continuous pressures the person faces, because of the long-term consequences of the exposure to pathogens and to endemic stressors (i.e., high vulnerability), and because of the chronic scarcity of services, resources and assets.[28]

It is not surprising, therefore, that one possible causal factor of the increased suicide rate among young black males may be the high unemployment rate they experienced between the 1970s and the 1990s. And in terms of education as a steppingstone to future employment, blacks during the second half of the twentieth century experienced limited success in higher education. In the 1980s and 1990s, economic recession, followed by a political assault on affirmative action and open admissions policies, resulted in a shrinking of opportunities for higher education for millions of black youth. In the early 1980s, the United Negro College Fund reported a significant decrease in the number of black college freshman, a trend that continued into the 1990s despite a growth in the total number of black high school graduates.[29] Overall, despite a booming economy during much of the 1990s, many black children were unable to attend college because of financial hardship, while others fell victim to poor preparation at inferior schools.

By the late 1990s, many black youth who made it to young adulthood faced a new set of difficulties—the prospect of building a life without the benefit of a meaningful education and without employment that would allow them to live above the poverty level. The outcome of this equation is the development of a pervasive sense of hopelessness among many young blacks. This hopelessness also fosters rage that at times is expressed in self-destructive behaviors.

Many young blacks surveying the landscape in the late 1990s saw around them desolation–poverty, crime, drugs–and the prospect of dependence on dwindling government assistance or underground economies for income. For many, their only contact with authority figures occurred in direct confrontations with police and other law enforcement or legal officials. For some, an entire set of negative effects that result from having a criminal record was added to their experience, a stacking up of problems which might be expected to increase the sense of despair and entrapment.

The precise connection between incarceration and suicide is difficult to document, but some research has been conducted in this area. According to Warren Breed's 1970 study in New Orleans, nearly 50 percent of the black males who committed suicide had a history of conflict with local authorities, particularly with the police, while only 10 percent of the white suicide victims in that city had had similar experiences.[30] (Indeed, both Carl Burton and Kenneth Poussaint had numerous run-ins with the law in the years before their deaths.) We do know that the possibility of suicide or suicidal behavior increases after individuals come into contact with the criminal justice system.

Not surprisingly, the subject of jail suicides is controversial and politically unpopular; its occurrence is frequently underreported and sometimes the cause of survivor lawsuits. In 1989, researcher Lindsay Hayes of the Massachusetts-based National Center on Institutions and Alternatives (NCIA) estimated that suicide was the leading cause of death in American jails.[31] A 1986 study of jail suicides by Hayes's group for the U.S. Justice Department's National Institute of Corrections found that the suicide rate in detention facilities was roughly nine times greater than the suicide rate of the general population. African-American men accounted for 16 percent of 401 jail suicides in the NCIA's 1986 study of suicides that were reported in county and local jails nationwide.[32] This information is particularly significant when one considers that black men represent about half of the nation's prison population. In 1997, according to the Sentencing Project in Washington, D.C., blacks comprised 51 percent of the state and federal prison population.[33] Moreover, blacks are arrested and jailed three to five times more often than whites.

In 1969, researcher R. W. Maris, looking at young blacks in Chicago in conflict with institutional authorities, concluded that the black suicides he studied were the result of retroflexed–anger turned inward–rather than of despair. In his study, he interpreted these suicides as reactions to social crises–imprisonment, arrest, breaking up with a spouse or girlfriend.[34] And, as Hayes of the NCIA noted in a 1989 article in the *Psychiatric Quarterly*,[35] several other elements have emerged as possible motivators or facilitators of jail suicides, including drug abuse or excessive drinking, recent loss of personal stability, guilt or shame, sexual assault or the threat of sexual assault, mental illness, poor health, or the reaching of an emotional breaking point. Some jail suicides may also reflect the dynamics of fatalistic suicide discussed earlier. It is quite possible that black men experience these negative outcomes in disproportionately higher numbers than whites, much as blacks are more likely to be the victims of crimes.

The relationship between black males, crime, incarceration, and suicide cannot be overlooked. Indeed, some investigators feel that the rage felt by black youth can manifest itself in either suicide or homicide. Homicide is the leading cause of death among young black men, accounting for approximately one-fifth of the deaths in late adolescence during most of the 1980s and 1990s. Suicide rates among young black males still lag behind the total homicide rate, but the suicide gap between young white males and young blacks is narrowing.

Some social scientists have speculated that the homicide rate varies inversely with the suicide rate in a given community. In the United States, homicide among nonwhites occurs from seven to ten times more frequently than it does among whites. In South Africa, the homicide rate among blacks is four times higher than the rate among whites, but the white suicide rate is four times higher than the black rate. In 80 to 90 percent of the homicides in the United States, the victim and the offender belong to the same ethnic group. In other words, one could speculate that the suicide rate in black communities would increase if the number of homicides decreased. There is no way of conclusively testing this hypothesis. Moreover, during the past sixty years, suicide and homicide rates in this country have varied independently and, in the black community, both rates have increased over time.

Other social scientists have explored the possibility that some black homicides are "victim-precipitated" and therefore represent a form of suicide. This theory is in keeping with the general impression that blacks are more likely than whites to be involved in various types of self-destructive behavior. Some observers conclude that urban riots are a form of community suicide in which the loss of black lives and black-owned businesses is far greater than the damage done to the white power structure. Others have commented that the Black Panthers and similar militant African-American political groups were on a suicidal quest, that they seemed intent on provoking law enforcement authorities to kill them. The problem with such speculations is that they often arise from unconscious—or conscious—attempts to blame the victims for the brutal acts of others.

The proliferation of guns, drugs, and crime, and the further fragmenting of the black family during the second half of the twentieth century are all pieces of the puzzle presented by the increasing suicide rate of African-Americans, particularly males. But again, the beginning of an understanding of the factors behind the current increase doesn't explain why, despite their hardships, the suicide rate among blacks has been significantly lower than that among whites for decades. We have discussed the argument that blacks are better able than whites to adjust to adversity because the fortitude and endurance necessary for survival have been nurtured by their art, culture, and religious institutions for centuries, as embodied in folklore and in grief-laden gospel, spiritual, and blues songs: "Nobody Knows the Troubles I've Seen," "Sometimes I Feel Like a Motherless Child," "The Down-Hearted Blues."

From the cradle to the pulpit to the grave, many blacks are taught that suffering on earth leads to great rewards in the afterlife. There are undoubtedly exceptions, but in the Christian beliefs adopted by most African-Americans, expectations of life and death are in many ways different from those of white. A tragedy that might drive a white man to self-murder might be accepted by a black man as merely one more episode in a life of hard times. That this high degree of resilience may now play a part in black reluctance to seek mental health counseling is worth considering. Where, for example, does a psychologically troubled young black man or woman turn when his or her family and peer group speaks only of "being strong" in the face of problems, especially if the clinical professional community is unfriendly and/or insensitive?

Further, many blacks—particularly those living in isolated low-income communities—have a unique attitude to so-called deviant behavior. Many blacks recognize that antisocial behavior is sometimes necessary for survival; and, while not expressly condoning it, many are likely to tacitly accept such behavior. Thus a black man who is a numbers runner or a street-level drug dealer is not likely to be permanently stigmatized in his neighborhood, while a white businessman convicted of embezzlement may be unprepared for the enduring scorn he is likely to face in his community. This kind of acceptance is understood to have a downside as well: black criminal activity, which often leads to incarceration, has in some parts of the black community become a fact of life.

All this may be true, but what else would account for the disparity?

Some writers and researchers have reported that blacks are less likely to become psychotically depressed and therefore are less suicidal than whites, citing the fact that for most of the twentieth century, in the Deep South the white rate of hospitalization for psychotic depression was four times higher than the black rate. But blacks, particularly in "whites only" environments, had difficulty gaining hospital admissions, especially to private institutions. Several studies have found low incidences of depression among blacks, but this conclusion may be due, at least in part, to bias on the part of white researchers who hold impressions of blacks as "happy-go-lucky." Some reports show that whites with serious mental disorders are likely to be diagnosed as having depressive illnesses, while blacks are more likely to be diagnosed with other psychotic disorders.[36]

Many clinical professionals assume that depression must be low in blacks simply *because* for so many decades the suicide rate of blacks was less than half that of whites. This raises questions, however, about the influence of history and cultural myths on investigators' thinking. If physicians generally perceive blacks as "happy" though downtrodden, what is the likelihood that they would identify depression in an African-American patients if they saw it? Perhaps what looks like a twenty-year increase in black male suicide is as much a function of late-coming awareness of biases in the medical community and of improved reporting methods as it is of any cultural or psychological factors that might be propelling a true increase.

Whatever part white bias plays, it has been consistently reported that severe depressive illness afflicts fewer black Africans than North American blacks. Some investigators believe that early intensive mothering in African groups, and willingness to satisfy a child's strong early nurturing needs serves to stave off the development of depressive illnesses. Another theory holds that like some African communities which provide strong, nurturing bonds that decrease individual loneliness and isolation, black Americans share an extended family in which kinship bonds are strong and many relatives are available to love and support an individual in distress.[37] Within the past twenty years, this argument continues, a breakdown in traditional black American family life has produced a host of serious problems, including a rise in drug use, teen motherhood, and crime, along with educational setbacks.

Some psychiatrists have suggested that blacks in America suffer from chronic despair as a reaction to racist oppression, and we know that despair—the loss of hope—is a major risk factor for self-destructive behavior, from the overt act of leaping to one's death or shooting oneself to long-form, indirect suicide through unhealthy lifestyles (excessive drinking, drug abuse, and, in the age of AIDS, risky sexual behavior). Therefore, an examination of the impact of America's history of white racism—both on the mental health of blacks and on black skepticism toward the medical community—is essential to the nationwide effort to understand and prevent African-American suicide.

3

"Boy, You Must Be Crazy"

Racism's Historic Impact on
Black Physical and Mental Health

African-American skepticism toward the medical and mental health care communities has deep roots in our nation's history. Before we identify and examine the factors currently contributing to blacks' wariness of the medical community–or analyze further the reluctance of blacks to admit mental distress and the ways in which that reluctance may contribute to self-destructive behavior–we must first review the historic relationship in which whites defined, from the days of slavery onward, what was normal behavior for African-Americans. Those blacks whose behavior failed to fit the self-serving needs of the white supremacist perspective were deemed "crazy" or "dangerous." These and similar labels were particularly likely to be placed on blacks who rebelled against slavery or refused to comply with the oppressive system that followed it.

The legacy of hundreds of years of official misrepresentation and misinterpretation of black behavior is a morass of harmful myths and stereotypes about African-Americans' behavior and mental health, including faulty beliefs that have been internalized by blacks themselves–with devastating results.

We must not forget that for more than two hundred years in America, the prevailing definitions of what was "normal" for blacks were based on conceptual observations formed and disseminated by whites who viewed blacks as inferior and who benefited from keeping blacks powerless. Americans, black and white, are still struggling to cast off the brutish imagery and primitive mythology created by these eighteenth- and nineteenth-century representations.

At the beginning of the twentieth century, to cite a particularly egregious example, one psychologist stated that using the same treatments for different races was equivalent to applying the same veterinary practices to different animal species.[1] Racists asserted that the black brain was smaller and less developed than the white's, and therefore blacks were not capable of managing a high degree of civilization. And as late as the 1960s there were some white psychiatrists practicing in Mississippi (for example) who would not see black patients. Even more recently, some white psychiatrists have aligned themselves with racist policies and used so-called objective psychiatric concepts to support their positions.

In 1965, coauthor Alvin Poussaint was witness to a group of white psychiatrists in Mississippi who opposed the integration of their all-white hospital unit by saying they believed "it would be bad for the mental health of both whites and blacks." These mental health clinicians seemed either blind or cunning in not appreciating that their position meant both maintaining the social status quo and not providing services for black people—and that this exclusionary outlook flew in the face of the Hippocratic oath. Many of them started to accept black patients only after the Civil Rights Act of 1964 was enforced by the federal government, and initially, following their racist etiquette, they only admitted black women as inpatients because black women were thought to be less of a "threat" than black men. Here again, the history of racism, particularly the white fear of blacks as hypersexual and animalistic, contributed to the neglect of black mental patients; these white Southerners were particularly afraid to break the racist taboo by allowing black men to socialize with white women on their inpatient units. In this situation, it's easy to recognize how the practice of psychiatry vis-à-vis blacks was closely linked to the politics of racism.

Indeed, the mistrust of the medical establishment that currently contributes to poor mental health in some blacks can be linked to the long history of troubled relations between blacks and the whole American medical community. An honest look at that history reveals patterns of neglect and cases of unethical and occasionally abusive practices by white doctors, medical students, and clinicians which help explain why some African-

Americans continue to believe that a genocidal plan has been at work. The shape of this belief ranges from the possibility that AIDS was invented by government scientists seeking to decimate the black population to long-held fears among some blacks that many of the nation's official institutions are working—in ways subtle and overt—to eliminate or to keep them in peril. Aside from the question of whether the current facts support these beliefs, it is important to consider that many black Americans view the medical and mental health care communities as coconspirators in a political and social system that was designed to obstruct black progress. And such beliefs, accumulated over many decades, add a psychic burden to the collective mindset of black Americans, one that has no counterpart among whites.

The earliest writings by white doctors on black psychology and physiology are unmistakably products of their times. At least since the nineteenth century, observations and descriptions of blacks by white, predominantly Southern doctors influenced the clinical canon that was later used by some clinicians to interpret and diagnose black behavior and illness.

That early white researchers carried racist beliefs—often supported by pseudoscience—has led to troubling shortcomings in the education of generations of American psychologists and psychiatrists. As black psychologist William A. Hayes of Tennessee noted in a 1972 collection, *Black Psychology,* the annals of American psychiatric literature are "replete with attempts to explain black behavior . . . by resorting to hypothetical mental structures, presumed needs, attitudes and the like. Because these so-called explanations go beyond observable events, they are conceptualizations of behavior rather than explanations of behavior."[2]

Much of what the early medical doctors "conceptualized" about black behavior was based on a core of racist stereotypes and assumptions. In sum, the concept of "normal" black physiology and psychology as defined by early white medical and mental health experts held that blacks were physically and intellectually inferior to whites, and, conveniently for their oppressors, destined to be slaves. Blacks who acted outside of the accepted norm, that is, who failed to acquiesce to being actual or virtual slaves, were seen by some nineteenth-century white doctors as belligerent, as possibly suffering from mental illness, and ultimately as dangerous.

Well into the twentieth century, conventional wisdom within the medical-scientific establishment about the physical and mental condition of blacks was still based on ideological formations forged during the years

when slavery–America's "peculiar institution"–was accepted as "normal"
by much of the U.S. population. And throughout our history, the mental and
physical well-being of black Americans has rarely been a priority for political or medical leaders, beyond blacks' ability to produce sufficient work for
the labor requirements of a given era.

"The history of racism has . . . intersected in several ways with the history of mental health care," wrote Castellano B. Turner and Bernard
Kramer in their 1995 book *Mental Health, Racism, and Sexism.* "Racism is
implicated . . . in the formulation of theories of mental health and illness.
Theories about the origins of mental illness range from those that are biological in nature (genetic predisposition, biochemical imbalance, and so
on) to those that view mental illness primarily as a social construction."[3]
And during the earliest days of medical research in America, conscious
efforts were made to "prove" the mental capacities of blacks to be inferior to
those of whites.

In the 1800s, a small but prolific group of Southern doctors–perhaps to
counter the antislavery sentiments that gave birth to the abolitionist movement–began producing professional papers arguing that blacks were, in
effect, suited to serve in bondage and living happily under the system of
slavery. During the five decades before the Civil War, a time when the South
depended on slave labor to sustain its place in the nation's burgeoning economy, the medical-scientific community continued to provide "expert" opinion that blacks were inferior to whites by nearly every measure. Above all,
blacks were portrayed as mentally inferior to whites, more akin to lower
forms of hominids than to modern human beings. Not only did this thinking enable whites to morally justify keeping blacks in bondage, it also allowed a small number of doctors to use blacks for questionable medical experiments both before and long after the Civil War.

Popular cultural outlets–from newspapers, to magazines to professional
journals and, in the early twentieth century, motion pictures–perpetuated
images of blacks as emotionally uncomplicated, childlike individuals, usually either sullen and angry, as in D. W. Griffith's 1915 cinematic landmark,
Birth of a Nation, or faithful to their white masters and cheerily resigned
to their slave status, as was Uncle Tom in Harriet Beecher Stowe's 1852
melodramatic book *Uncle Tom's Cabin.* Furthermore, popular nineteenth-
century American culture often depicted blacks as falling outside of all that
which was ostensibly good, clean, pure and "normal"; in the view of many

whites, blacks came to be seen as dirty and animalistic. (The so-called science that supported the political and economic institution of slavery mollified any guilt or sense of injustice that perhaps would have developed in whites who were not directly tied to slavery.)

An utter dearth of objective analyses of blacks' physical and cultural uniqueness—of analyses that took into consideration the fact that blacks were forced to remain economically and politically powerless—created an atmosphere in which some whites applied a host of traits, physical and mental, to define what was "normal" for blacks. Concepts promulgated by some white doctors, researchers, and Christian leaders described blacks in a taxonomy that was infantilizing and intellectually narrow: with few exceptions, blacks were said to be childlike, docile, superstitious, gifted with preternatural physical strength, devoted to a strict but merciful God, and mostly complacent within their enslaved status—"happy-go-lucky" in the face of unceasing hard labor, domestic servitude, and stinging cruelties such as whipping, sexual abuse, and lynching.

In a social system supported by the courts, politicians, and legal and medical scholars, blacks who protested slavery or otherwise rebelled against the accepted order faced beatings or death. Those who attempted to run away from white plantations were said to suffer from mental illness, with one particularly creative Southern doctor coining the damning term "drapetomania" (runaway mania)[4] to describe the mental condition of blacks who ran away and escaped to freedom. In this bizarre, pseudo-scientific twist, blacks who did not accept the norm of being enslaved and who wanted freedom were seen as suffering from various forms of psychopathology.

After the Civil War, through Reconstruction and the Jim Crow, pre–civil rights eras of the mid-twentieth century, blacks who failed to comply with the near-feudal sharecropping system or abide by the lopsided rules of a white-dominated racial hierarchy continued to be viewed by some whites as "troublemakers" or "crazy niggers," dangerous individuals who threatened the status quo or the "natural" state of black-white relations.

In the intervening decades, white perceptions of black mental health, and what constitutes "healthy" behavior, has moved somewhat closer to reality (today relatively few whites, for example, would admit to believing that blacks are not human beings). But although social and political progress and advancements in scientific and medical research have officially dispelled many of the old myths, the result of centuries' worth of medical misinformation and harmful practices has led to a deeply turbulent relationship between the medical establishment and many black Americans.

This relationship has improved over the years, but a look back provides a bleak history lesson. For many decades following the abolishment of slavery, the segregation of public and private institutions and businesses—including hospitals not only in the Deep South but also and in other parts of the United States—combined with a lack of black doctors to create a vacuum in which millions of African-Americans were denied voluntary access to routine medical care. Even in the North, black patients were often treated in poorly funded and understaffed hospitals in urban ghettoes, resulting in poor care and higher death rates. Often, de facto segregation in health care in the North mirrored the de jure segregation and discrimination against blacks in the South.

As a result, black contact with the medical establishment was often limited to emergency situations or involuntary hospitalizations that often ended unhappily for the patient. Not surprisingly, many blacks came to see doctors—particularly white doctors and psychiatrists—as threatening and authoritarian figures. Furthermore, blacks heard and passed on stories of mistreatment, incarceration, and unspeakable modes of experimentation—and some of these stories were essentially true. At the twilight of the twentieth century, many black Americans cited the same egregious example of professional abuse to explain why they continued to harbor suspicions about the predominantly white health care establishment: the Tuskegee syphilis study.[5]

Beginning in 1932, teams of government researchers conducted a long-term study of the effects of syphilis on a group of black men in Alabama. It ran for more than forty years. The study began with good intentions but eventually went horribly awry. Although an antibiotic treatment for syphilis was developed in the 1940s, the researchers withheld the medicines, and without the knowledge or consent of dozens of black men they allowed the disease to run its course in them, with fatal results in some cases. Now, twenty-five years after its exposure in the national media, the story of the Tuskegee syphilis study has grown in the minds of many black Americans as the prime symbol of how the medical and scientific communities abuse and neglect African-Americans.

Over the years, the details of the Tuskegee study have been embellished with misinformation, including the mistaken belief that some of the men used in the study were injected with syphilis (they were not). Such confusion has served to further muddy the waters where blacks and the health care establishment are concerned. Yet even before that now infamous forty-year study, blacks in America were the subjects of numerous other cruel practices and unethical experiments.

In one example from the antebellum era, a Georgia medical doctor named Thomas Hamilton, who was trying to develop medication to treat the effects of heat stroke, placed a male slave named Fed in a covered pit with only his head exposed; for several days, Fed was given different compounds in an effort to determine which of the remedies were effective. After each dose, Fed fainted and had to be revived so the experiment could continue, according to Dr. Vanessa Northington Gamble of the Center for the Study of Race and Ethnicity in Medicine at the University of Wisconsin School of Medicine.

Obviously, Dr. Hamilton's first priority was not to safeguard the welfare of his slave, and there is no way of knowing if his treatment of Fed was viewed by other blacks who heard of it as legitimate medical experimentation or cruelty and abuse. It is not hard to imagine, however, that news of this and similar incidents spread through the local black population, giving rise to a not unreasonable fear of white medical doctors.

In a 1997 report in the *American Journal of Public Health*,[6] Northington Gamble recounts the story of Fed and Dr. Hamilton, along with other instances of black Southerners undergoing similar treatment and worse at the hands of white Southern doctors and researchers—usually under the guise of a great humanitarian effort to further our understanding of the body and the diseases that prey on it.

Following the Civil War, according to the same author, black graveyards were sometimes used by administrators of white medical schools as an easily accessible resource for cadavers: in some quarters, cottage industries developed wherein black people's bodies were exhumed—without the consent of living relatives—and sold by white graveyard owners to medical schools for a profit. Northington Gamble also describes African-American folktales dating to the turn of the century detailing black fears of "night doctors"—whites who were believed to kidnap blacks at night, kill them, and use them for medical experiments. And, as chronicled in Gladys-Marie Fry's book *Night Riders in Black Folk History*, blacks in South Carolina in the late 1890s lived in fear of a white man who reportedly "made himself invisible," used chloroform to subdue unsuspecting blacks, then drew buckets of blood from the victims before dumping their bodies in a remote area.[7]

Not all stories of abuse by white doctors and researchers fell under the rubric of folklore or represented isolated incidents. In fact, black men and women were routinely experimented on, often with disastrous results. Between 1845 and 1849, for example, Dr. J. Marion Sims, an Alabama physician who conducted early gynecological research, used three black women slaves in an experiment to learn how to repair vaginal irregularities. During that five-year period the three women underwent more than thirty painful surgical operations without the aid of anesthesia; after the procedure was fine-tuned, Sims used it to treat white patients. As Northington Gamble has noted, the small community of black medical doctors in the early twentieth century were so angered by experimentation on African-Americans by whites, and by other discriminatory medical practices, that they began pushing for the formation of black-controlled hospitals.

Widespread anecdotal evidence, combined with published writings by medical doctors from the nineteeth and early twentieth centuries, shows again and again how the conventional medical wisdom surrounding blacks and black mental health also came to be shaped by racist assumptions and beliefs.

From the antebellum era through the early twentieth century, "a prominent explanation of mental illness has been that of genetic predisposition in some racial stocks," Turner and Kramer wrote in 1995. "An alleged indication of such inferiority was the presumed 'scientifically demonstrated' prevalence of mental inferiority and mental illness in that population."[8] In other words, black inferiority was believed to be the norm; blacks were seen as innately "deficient" in general when compared with whites, making African-Americans fair game for a host of half-baked studies and experiments in the mental health arena, and to classification by a system of questionable terminology.

In the Deep South during the pre–Civil War years, a handful of medical doctors (many also slave owners) came to be known as de facto "experts" on the black mind-set. Dr. Samuel A. Cartwright, the Louisiana surgeon and psychologist who coined the term "drapetomania" in 1851, described blacks as being predisposed to carrying out hard work. He also identified them as being docile, childlike, and simple-minded by nature. Should their owners attempt to work blacks too hard, Cartwright warned, "they invariably do less and less, until they fall into a state of impassivity, in which they are more plague than profit—worthless as laborers, insensible and indifferent to punishment or even to life."

Writing in 1857 in *The Ethnology of the Negro or the Prognathous Race,* Cartwright continued, "They fall into the disease which I have named dysaesthesia Aethiopica, characterized by hebetude of mind and insensitivity of body, caused by overworking and bad treatment."[9]

According to historian Eugene Genovese in his seminal look at the lives of black slaves in America, *Roll Jordan, Roll,* Cartwright and other white doctors like Josiah Nott and John Stainback Wilson declared that blacks could be depended on to do well in plodding, physically demanding jobs but were ill-equipped mentally to handle work that was intellectually rigorous.[10]

Blacks were also believed to be suspicious and superstitious by nature and, with few exceptions, untrustworthy and sexually promiscuous. At the same time, white doctors continued to describe blacks as being imbued with an acquiescent disposition that allowed them to accept their plight as unpaid forced laborers; William McDougall, an eminent psychologist in 1908, wrote that the Negro race had an "instinct of submission."[11] Nearly a half-century after emancipation, blacks who demonstrated "rebelliousness"—or even independent or critical thinking skills—were still often thought of as "crazy," or at the very least as "not knowing their place."

These patriarchal and often contradictory views of blacks extended into other areas of whites' perceptions, including the belief that blacks could never be happy in the North. Some white doctors maintained that blacks in the North suffered from high instances of psychological problems because they had dared to move "out of their place"; they saw themselves as benevolent protectors, conscientious professionals, as they argued that segregation helped shield blacks from mental illness, depression, and suicide. Moreover, Cartwright and his intellectual compatriots held fast to the notion that only Southern doctors could effectively treat blacks. The extent to which such biases and "scientific" theories—recorded for posterity in professional journals in the Deep South and later in certain national medical journals—continue to indirectly influence white medical educators is open to question.

The distortion and devaluation of black lives by the nation's institutions and by many white individuals is a legacy of slavery that continues to impact negatively on African-Americans' health and their relationship with the medical-scientific community.

While it is difficult to gauge the full extent to which black Americans may have internalized public and institutional racism, one could argue that the medical, scientific, and psychiatric communities have played a continuing role in contributing to poor self-perception among many African-Americans. A black person struggling with questions of self-worth (as many individuals do at some point in their lives) has only to look at the many ways that blacks were and are abused by the medical community—as well as the courts, employers and merchants, and other sectors of American society—to reinforce a sense of self-doubt. Historically, few blacks were in a position to question the accepted definition of normalcy, or challenge whites who would attach the label "crazy" to an African-American seeking to buck the status quo.

As a result of a belief system affirmed over the years by the kind of "scholarship" we've reviewed, blacks who posed a real or imagined threat to white authority could find themselves jailed or, in some regions, committed to poorly funded and/or segregated state mental institutions, places that deserved to be called "snake pits." Even today in the parlors and porches of some black Southern homes, relatives tell of loved ones who disappeared into the bowels of such institutions.

In the past, many of the white psychiatrists responsible for overseeing these facilities tended to view black mental health issues in simplistic terms, if they considered them at all. Most state hospitals in the Deep South were segregated until the late 1960s, when the federal government forced their integration and the hiring of black doctors as part of the funding requirements of the Civil Rights Act of 1964. Prior to that time, the few black wards in these facilities were outfitted with castoff furnishings and equipment, and staffed by workers with minimal training; even in the North, blacks with mental illness were usually relegated to state hospitals where they often received biased and inadequate care.

And, in an example of the tenacious nature of segregated life, even following the official integration of hospitals nationwide, in the South many blacks declined to partake of previously whites-only facilties for fear of retribution by white workers. During a visit to a county hospital in Mississippi during the late 1960s, coathor Alvin Poussaint spoke with black patients who continued to sit in the waiting room area that for many decades had been designated "colored only." When he asked them why, they replied that they didn't want to anger white hospital staff members for fear that some might vindictively withhold care or even just let them die.

In the North, the hospitals most accessible to blacks, like Chicago's Provident, were underfunded shadows of their white counterparts. Tales of blacks being undertreated or mistreated abounded, and many hospitals in the North expected blacks to submit to research as a payback for "charity" or free care. But it was worse in the South. There were many reports, for instance, of Southern black women in the end stages of labor being turned away from "whites only" hospitals and left to give birth in precarious situations like automobiles, or in their homes aided by a black midwife called hastily to the scene. In addition, in both the South and the North, before informed consent was instituted in the 1950s, blacks continued to be used as research subjects without their permission or knowledge.

The abuse of blacks by the medical establishment did not end with the death of legalized segregation. In parts of the Deep South, for example, the practice of routinely sterilizing black women who were admitted to the hospital for other operations continued into the early 1970s, according to Dorothy Roberts, a Northwestern University law professor and author of *Killing the Black Body* (1995).[12] This came to be known among blacks as a "Mississippi appendectomy." Civil rights activist Fannie Lou Hamer, a sharecropper who mobilized poor blacks in the heart of the Delta, reported that as a young adult she was given an unnecessary hysterectomy without her consent by a white physician. Before her death in 1977, she explained to her biographer, Kay Mills, that the experience had helped radicalize her.[13]

In the mental health arena, doctors had the power to order the involuntary hospitalization of an individual without the procedural safeguards that have since been put in place to prevent abuse of that power. For many blacks, involuntary commitment to state institutions was equivalent to being jailed. Even today, stories of traumatic experiences with mental health care providers in the past evoke a fear that white psychiatric personnel will misuse their authority at the expense of black freedom. (Although, in fairness, where involuntary hospitalization in state mental facilities is concerned, the absence of an appropriate consent process was occasionally ex-

ploited by blacks as well: disputes over property, child custody, or marital
matters sometimes led blacks to accuse each other of mental instability–
and to summon white authorities to involuntarily commit their spouse or
family member to a mental institution).

Over time, however, overt racism was being challenged, American society
was changing, and such abuses became fewer. As the struggle for equal
rights for blacks grew into the civil rights movement, the scientific community underwent a theoretical shift from one-dimensional definitions of
blacks and their mental health toward a view that black Americans suffered
from mental stress and illness as a "mark of oppression."

This latter phrase was coined by psychiatrists Abram Kardiner and Lionel Ovesey in their 1951 work of the same name, which was based on a psychoanalytic study of twenty-five black patients (a rather small sample).
Kardiner and Ovesey argued that black Americans bear a unique set of psychic scars that result directly from constant exposure to racism and discrimination, that all black Americans suffer from this "mark of oppression," and that there were no "black personality traits" that could not be
traced to the effects of difficulties wrought by white racism. They saw no exceptions to this rule and concluded that "the Negro has no possible basis for
a healthy self-esteem and every incentive for self-hatred."[14] They failed to
note any healthy aspects of the black cultural experience and saw attempts
by blacks to identify as Afro-Americans as manifestation of self-hatred
rather than positive affirmations of self-worth. Despite obvious flaws, the
theories of Kardiner and Ovesey represented a willingness on the part of
mental health professionals to look at black life in new ways.

In 1954, in its landmark decision to ban de jure segregated schools as un-
constitutional, the United States Supreme Court cited the groundbreaking
studies begun in 1939 by Kenneth Clark and Mamie Clark, pioneering black
psychologists who explored the negative effects of racism on the self-image
of black children. In one study, recording the reactions of young Southern
black children to white and black dolls, they had found that children from
segregated environments generally had negative reactions to the black
dolls and positive reactions to the white ones.[15]

The arrival of the Black Power cultural and political movement in the
1960s coincided with an effort among black mental health clinicians to re-
examine the language of mental health and redefine what constituted nor-

mal black behavior, marking the onset of a politicization of black health issues that is only lately beginning to gain the attention of the black population. Black clinicians challenged concepts that still subtly defined blacks as deficient versions of whites, as epitomized in phrases like "culturally deprived," used by white clinicians to explain black social and psychological pathology. Black psychiatrists and psychologists, using new perspectives, argued that blacks suffered conditions such as depression and paranoia, just as whites do, and linked antisocial behaviors with the devastating impact of white racism on the black psyche. White clinicians were challenged to examine their own prejudices and the psychopathologies in white Americans that have often driven them to brutal, uncaring, and racist practices against blacks. The new formulations about "black consciousness" that arose in the 1960s and 1970s looked at much black behavior as culturally different rather than culturally deficient with regard to white-derived norms.

As blacks gained access to the full range of institutions of higher learning where doctors are trained (beyond Howard and Meharry, historically segregated black schools), the difference between black clinicians' views of black mental health and white clinicians' views became—as it still is—politically volatile, especially with regard to the ongoing debate over disparities in funding for minority health and education programs.

In the 1960s, through articles in professional journals and debate in academic circles, a small community of black medical doctors, psychiatrists, and psychologists (including coauthor Alvin Poussaint) began loudly challenging historic precepts about black behavior and black health. In 1968, psychiatrists William Grier and Price Cobbs argued in their book *Black Rage*[16] that as a result of slavery and crushing discrimination, blacks suffered from "cultural paranoia," and that because of their historic intimacy with misery and grief they had developed a "cultural depression," a form of general malaise that derived from being outsiders in their own country.

They were building on the work of a handful of black social scientists, psychologists, and psychiatrists like Charles Prudhomme, author of a 1938 paper on black suicide;[17] E. Franklin Frazier, author of controversial books on the black middle-class, who had laid the groundwork for black-oriented clinical psychology studies;[18] and, of course, Kenneth Clark, who inspired many other black psychologists and psychiatrists to address both the impact of racism on the black psyche and the problem of institutionalized racism.[19]

In 1963, Frantz Fanon, a black psychiatrist living in Algeria, revolutionized the thinking of many black mental health professionals—and that of intellectuals the world over—with the publication of *The Wretched of the Earth*, a book that challenged archaic racial constructs and called for new ways of assessing and defining the psychology of the black experience.[20] Fanon wrote of the deep dehumanizing effects of European colonialism on oppressed people of color around the world. He felt that the colonial neuroses of the oppressed are best overcome through activism (including violence) rather than passive resistance. Fanon was widely popular among U.S. black militants (particularly the Black Panthers) in the 1960s and 1970s; many cited his work to argue that violence toward white racists in self-defense was "therapeutic" for the black masses. Anathema to the white power structure, Fanon's writings provided the theoretical underpinning for revolutionary movements against colonialism worldwide, particularly on the continent of Africa.

The influential collection *Black Psychology,* published in 1972 and edited by psychologist Reginald L. Jones, contained scholarly papers by black psychiatrists, social workers, medical doctors, and psychologists, and raised key questions about the influence of white racism on black emotional well-being and about racial bias in the diagnostic tools used to assess mental health.[21] (Nearly twenty years later, in 1990, much of the same territory was revisited in *The Handbook of Mental Health and Mental Disorder among Black Americans,* a scholarly collection edited by Dorothy Ruiz that updated black mental health diagnostic and treatment issues.)[22]

These professional writings represent a particularly American subspecialty of psychology that has received little attention within the larger field in comparison to the theories and practices of white American and European psychiatrists and doctors. And outside the clinical, research, and academic communities, relatively few Americans, black or white, have viewed the reading of such philosophical and clinical material as a top priority. What tends to matter most to ordinary citizens, regardless of their race, are the mundane, visceral, and tangible aspects of life, as well as the accumulated experiences of their families and friends.

But history's hold on the collective consciousness of blacks and whites is impressively strong. Even as the changes of the '50s, '60s, and '70s took hold, the presence of racial bias–however subliminal, however benign–continued to shape policy and research on blacks as found in the nation's preeminent medical and science journals, including the *New England Journal of Medicine* and the *Journal of the American Medical Association.* For example, a 1971 article in the *Journal of the American College of Obstetrics and Gynecology* by Arthur T. Fort, a white doctor, recommended that black women showing traits of sickle cell anemia should be sterilized.[23] And no one seems to have questioned a research project by University of Texas doctors who had deprived at least 12 black infants of linoleic acid, a fatty substance essential for their development, during a 1956 study.[24] Some of the infants, who were subjected to this experiment without their parents' consent, developed severe skin rashes, respiratory infections, and other negative side effects as a result; this study was later repeated with a larger group of 428.[25]

Bias and racial insensitivity continue to affect patient care at all levels of the medical and psychiatric establishment, and has seeped into the fabric of America's health care apparatus, staining the ground-level service delivery systems with which black Americans must interact. Comprehensive studies are few, but since the 1950s surveys concerning black attitudes toward doctors and health care institutions have repeatedly revealed that many black Americans feel alienated by insensitive treatment on the part of medical workers and by an overall atmosphere of cultural intolerance. More important, the practices of some white clinicians may be influenced by a patient's race or gender.

The results of an investigation by researchers at Georgetown University, for example, raised questions about whether a majority of doctors hold prejudices which might prevent them from adequately treating all their patients. In a controlled study involving black and white patients suffering from heart trouble–patients whose income, education, and age levels were identical–the Georgetown researchers found that the 720 white doctors surveyed were less inclined to recommend early-stage preventive heart treatments, like angioplasty and catheterization, for black patients. "Our findings suggest that a patient's race and sex may influence a physician's recommendation with respect to cardiac catheterization regardless of the patient's clinical characteristics," they reported in 1999 in the *New England Journal of Medicine.* "The physicians' mean estimates of the probability of coronary artery disease were lower for women ... and blacks were less likely to be referred for cardiac catheterization than men and whites, respectively," wrote Kevin A. Schulman, one of the study's authors.[26]

This study also shed light on an important subtext of the minority health care gap in America–the impact of gender on diagnosis, treatment, and medical and mental health service delivery. "Analysis of race-sex interactions showed that black women were significantly less likely to be referred for catheterization than white men," the report continued, concluding with the statement: "Our findings suggest that the race and sex of a patient independently influence how physicians manage chest pain."[27]

And beyond the findings of the Georgetown study of physician attitudes, statistics show that blacks suffer disproportionately from treatable illnesses due to a combination of factors including low income, poor access to transportation and health care information, and cultural resistance to the medical establishment. In 1999, a partial list of health problems that negatively impact blacks in greater numbers than whites, and which could be ameliorated with early treatment, was telling:[28]

• African-Americans were 70 percent more likely than whites to suffer from diabetes, a disease which increases the risk for cardiovascular disease and blindness.

• The mortality rate for black babies, at 14.2 per 1,000 live births in 1996, was nearly two and a half times that of white babies.

• The death rate for African-American men with cancer was nearly 50 percent higher than for white men, about 226.8 deaths per 100,000, while the mortality rate from prostate cancer was more than twice that of white men, 55.5 deaths per 100,000.

• By 1998, more than 50 percent of new AIDS cases nationwide occurred among African-Americans, as did 63 percent of new cases among those between the age of thirteen and twenty-four years old–and blacks, particularly the poor, have much more difficulty in accessing and affording AIDS treatments than do whites.

In addition, in August 1999, a U.S. Centers for Disease Control and Prevention report raised the alarm about the high mortality rate for black women in childbirth: during the nine years between 1987 and 1996, one black woman died for every 5,102 who gave birth, compared with one in 18,868 whites.[29]

After the results of the Georgetown University study were published in the *New England Journal of Medicine,* black Americans had proof that their suspicions about unequal treatment from health care providers were justified. Yet health and science editors at many of the nation's largest news organizations scarcely blinked: whereas other large studies published by this prestigious journal routinely spur comprehensive coverage, no in-depth stories detailing the significant findings of the Georgetown study were printed in any of the Northeast's largest and most influential daily newspapers. In May of 1998, the *New York Times Sunday Magazine* published an article exposing the poor state of health services for the mentally ill in New York state, but its report did not examine the subject of race and mental health care.

While the past decade has seen a growing number of psychotherapists and medical experts acknowledge the troubling dearth of resources directed at minority health care issues–including the nation's second black U.S. surgeon general, David Satcher–increased awareness among the public and the political establishment has not followed.

The mainstream news media have not used their significant influence on public awareness, and consequently on the formation of public policy initiatives and funding, to address these issues; rather they have become complicit in perpetuating the myths and racial stereotypes which continue to keep the black mental health crisis out of the government funding pipeline. With few exceptions–notably in-depth series published in 1998 by *Newsday* and by the Knight-Ridder News Corporation's Washington bureau–the mainstream media do not appear to view the disparities in health care as an important concern. The rare story examining the minority health care gap, including the *New York Times* piece about the CDC report on the high mortality rate among pregnant black women, invariably tosses in language about blacks' historic reliance on God to solve secular problems like poor health, a simplistic approach that ignores the whole topic of black skepticism toward the medical establishment.

The rise in suicide among young black men during the two decades between 1980 and 1999 represents the tip of the iceberg of critical health issues facing black Americans, and no one advocates overlooking the important role that black self-determination must play in addressing them. Nevertheless, numerous studies show black Americans neglected in funding and lagging far behind in participation in medical programs and surveys, while blacks have one of the highest mortality rates in the nation.

In an interesting dichotomy, however much blacks avoid the mental health care community, they are more likely than whites to be diagnosed with serious illnesses should they be evaluated by clinicians. In 1980, for example, blacks made up 12 percent of the U.S. population but represented more than 18 percent of all hospital admissions nationwide, including admissions to mental hospitals and Veterans Administration medical centers, according to Dr. Sandra E. Taylor, coeditor of *Health Issues in the Black Community*, a 1992 compilation of black-oriented health care studies.[30]

In a larger cultural context, the widening minority health care gap is but one of several examples of how vestiges of white racism continue to infuse the black experience. Despite the well-documented gains blacks have made during the twentieth century in education, income, and other indicators of prosperity, African-Americans still fall prey to white discrimination in housing, employment, and the criminal justice system.

Beginning in the 1980s, vociferous attacks on affirmative action and public funding for programs perceived as "minority handouts" were launched by white conservatives supported by a small percentage of blacks, heightening the sense of oppression for many African-Americans. Moreover, the historic difference between what many whites consider to be black behavior (often stereotyped) and blacks' place in the social structure, and what blacks see as appropriate behavior on their part and their place in society, continues to be miles apart.

In *Rage of a Privileged Class*, a 1993 look at the frustrations of middle-class African-Americans, journalist Ellis Cose tells the stories of dozens of prominent and influential blacks who experience psychological stress that they attribute to remnants of white racism. In the course of his research, Cose found that millions of blacks who have "played by the white man's rules" and are educated, productive members of society are nevertheless frequently discriminated against by whites in nearly every aspect of life. "Why would people who have enjoyed all the fruits of the civil rights revolution—who have Ivy League educations, high-paying jobs, and comfortable homes—be quietly seething inside?" he asks. "To answer that question is to go a long way toward explaining why quotas and affirmative action remain such polarizing issues; why black and white Americans continue to see race in such starkly different terms; and why solving America's racial problems is infinitely more complicated than cleaning up the nation's urban ghettos and educating the inhabitants—even assuming the will, wisdom, and resources [exist] to accomplish such a task."[31]

Indeed, the reluctance of some whites to admit the validity of blacks' ongoing frustrations vis-à-vis race relations contributes to an overall sense of emotional isolation among many African-Americans. And for millions of blacks this sense of isolation is heightened by the great distance they see between themselves and the medical community.

Blacks in the 1990s were not being paranoid if they looked around and saw a nation that was still not entirely free of white racist practices. During the last decade of the twentieth century, black Americans experienced a bittersweet mix of high achievement (the proportion of middle-class blacks in America continues to increase; between 1967 and 1991, the number of black households earning $50,000 or more per year grew from 5.2 to 12.1 percent, according to U.S. Census figures)[32] and vivid reminders of how far they still have to go to attain across-the-board equality with the white population. In 1993 top executives at Texaco, a major energy company, were caught on audiotape making racist jokes and scheming to keep black workers out of the management ranks; in the 1990s several national fast-food chains were found to discriminate against blacks both as employees and as patrons; recently the government has found merit in a class-action suit filed by black farmers alleging discrimination by public agencies; and across the United States, taxis continue to avoid picking up black people, which causes considerable personal distress. In the minds of many black Americans, continuing evidence of white racism and oppression diminishes many of the lifestyle gains blacks have made.

The 1990s were, after all, a time when once again police brutality became a life-threatening concern for blacks and Latinos in much of the country. It was a decade in which law enforcement agencies around the United States came under scrutiny for racial profiling, the practice of detaining black or brown motorists because of the color of their complexions, for nothing more than "Driving While Black" (DWB) in the ironic phrase used by black citizens who had been through the experience; a decade in which a black man was dragged to his death behind a white neo-Nazi's pickup truck in Texas; a time when two New York City police officers were tried and found guilty of brutality after using a broomstick to sodomize a Haitian immigrant in a stationhouse bathroom; a time when four undercover New York City narcotics officers were indicted (but later acquitted by a jury) after firing forty-one bullets at an unarmed African immigrant, killing him on his own doorstep.

It was also a decade when blacks and other ethnic minorities continued to be left out of medical research projects. For example, in 1994 only 1.6 percent of the National Institute of Health's $60 million research budget went toward studying minority health, according to Dr. Moon Chen of Ohio State University's College of Medicine.[33]

The road to building a positive relationship between blacks and the medical establishment will be hard and bumpy. In 1998, Democratic president Bill Clinton unveiled a six-part plan to begin improving the state of minority health care in America. Called the Initiative to Eliminate Racial and Ethnic Disparities in Health, the $80 million plan is designed to address disparities in health care services and bring down high rates of diseases like diabetes, cancer, and HIV/AIDS among blacks by the year 2010. In 1999, the United States Congress voted to allocate $65 million of the $80 million for community-based programs in an effort that Surgeon General David Satcher says is needed to bring about "a real coming together of the public and private sectors."[34]

The specific nature of the proposed community programs is expected to take shape over several years, but to be successful they will have to address the cultural and historic factors that contribute to the minority health care gap. And among the many hurdles yet to be surmounted is the persistent presence of black reluctance to place a priority on seizing control over improving their own mental health.

Why, the thinking goes among many blacks, should we focus precious energy and resources on tackling the shadowy demons of mental health when we have so many other daunting hills to climb? Thus, while black skepticism of the medical community is understandable (based as it is on more than two hundred years' worth of anecdotal and documentary evidence), the stubborn reluctance of many blacks to address mental health concerns is trickier to pin down, though no less troubling.

For many blacks, the centuries-old fear of being tagged "crazy" by whites, has, over the decades between slavery and the post–civil rights era, turned into a deep fear of admitting emotional distress even to themselves. To do so conjures deeply held fears about appearing inferior, weak, or defective to whites and to one's own community. Blacks and whites in equal proportion suffer from a widespread stigmatization of mental illness, and even considering the late-1990s phenomenon of lurid public confessionals of the type found on some television talk shows and in other media, few Americans are eager to admit emotional problems for fear of being ostracized or discriminated against by the community at large or by friends, employers, and family members. In avoiding seeking regular medical checkups and preventive treatments, however, individual blacks ultimately jeopardize the future health of the African-American population.

As much as the medical establishment—the doctors, scientists, institutes, and organizations comprising the nation's health care community—must work harder to find better ways of treating and understanding black health concerns, African-Americans must work harder to begin overcoming their mistrust of medical practitioners, particularly mental health care providers. The growing crisis of depression, self-destructive behavior, and suicide among African-Americans cannot be effectively addressed until black political, scientific, and cultural leaders confront the stigma surrounding mental illness and begin encouraging blacks to overcome their historic trepidation toward the medical establishment and white physicians.

Today there are many white doctors, psychologists, and social workers who are ready to join hands with blacks to begin the hard work of change. At the same time, it is foolhardy to hold blacks solely responsible for mending their frayed relationship with the white-dominated medical and mental health care establishment. The government, as well as private health care providers, must do much more to acknowledge the truths of history that lie at the bottom of many blacks' distrust of the medical community, and they must work diligently and with innovative methods to make blacks feel welcome and secure in seeking medical care.

Any serious attempt to stem the rising suicide rates among blacks or close the minority health care gap must begin with honesty about our history as a nation and the complexity of the problems we face. The future mental health of America's black children depends on our ability to overcome the obstacles of that history in order to fulfill the nation's promise.

4

Hoping and Coping

Expectation versus Reality for African-Americans

Among the dominant risk factors for suicide–depression, a previous suicide attempt, drug or alcohol abuse, emotional isolation, access to firearms–hopelessness is a symptom that can be difficult to recognize or treat, but most clinical professionals agree that an individual who has lost hope for the future is greatly at risk for suicide or self-destructive, life-threatening behavior. Distinct from grief or the genetic and biological factors that can contribute to mental illness, hopelessness is a situational element that is frequently a strong indicator of clinical depression, and it is often linked to a sense of fatalism about the future. This can be particularly true for black youth mired in poverty-stricken communities.

In 1974, psychiatrist Aaron Beck devised a "Hopelessness Scale" designed to gauge hope's role as a "modulating variable linking depression and suicidal intent" in individuals.[1] In building his scale, Beck and his colleagues asked 294 hospitalized suicide attempters several questions designed to gauge "loss of motivation" and general feelings of pessimism. The patients were also asked to rate their responses to statements like "I can't imagine what my life would be like in ten years." Beck's work revealed that among these patients pessimistic thinking, combined with previous suicide attempts, was a reliable predictor of suicide in some cases. But hopelessness alone is not a consistent predictor, according to Anders Niméus and his co-authors in a 1997 paper on hopelessness and suicidal behavior.[2]

In 1995, psychologist Robert DuRant and his colleagues, using the hopelessness scale on a group of black children, reported that the adolescents they surveyed, who hailed from poor neighborhoods in Augusta, Georgia, and who were regularly exposed to community violence, exhibited high levels of hopelessness. DuRant's study found that those teenagers who believed they had little chance to reach the age of twenty-five also had higher depression scale scores.[3] Homicide is the leading cause of death for black men from ages fifteen to twenty-four, with a stunning homicide rate of about 85 per 100,000 in this age bracket: this reality no doubt contributes significantly to black youths' feelings of hopelessness in general when considering their chances for a brighter future. Succumbing to feelings of hopelessness has also been linked to alcohol and drug abuse, and other forms of self-destructive behavior. Except for the results of a few studies, much of what we know about hopelessness's impact on suicidal behavior in blacks is anecdotal or inferred from related psychological surveys of African-Americans and suicidal ideation. (The motives for suicide, of course, are complex, although most suicide victims are suffering from various psychiatric illnesses.) More clear are the methods generally employed by blacks for coping with psychological stress, including the social structures and supports they have erected to keep hopelessness and crippling pessimism at bay.

Throughout their time in America, blacks have drawn a sense of hope from spirituality and religion that positively affected their progress in this country. Unfortunately, today the involvement of blacks (particularly young black men) in church life has declined. This has weakened a support system that has historically been crucial to black survival.[4] Any comprehensive exploration of black suicide and self-destructive behavior should include an examination of the social context, including those institutions that have fostered hope in the community.

Within the context of the increase in black suicide rates since the early 1980s, it is likely that a loss of hope has played a significant role. Indeed, whether it predates mental illness or results from it, there is growing evidence that for millions of Americans, hopelessness, including a sense of being trapped by one's circumstances, undermines healthy emotional and psychological development. But determining the precise point at which hopelessness intersects with or precipitates mental illness, in blacks or other groups, is problematic. Although support systems such as church and family can soften the personal impact of many of life's stresses, even when strong components of religious/cultural and family-based beliefs exist, faith and hope fall short of being reliable, quantifiable influences on the overall state of one's mental health.

To paraphrase Supreme Court Justice Potter Stewart's famous observation about pornography, the average American knows hopelessness, especially in its most acute form, when he or she sees it. Since an estimated 18 million Americans currently suffer from a clinical depression,[5] it is clear to the average citizen that tragedies may result when individuals who have psychological or emotional problems lose hope. (For those who commit suicide believing they will be transported to some form of utopia, it is not clear if they are experiencing feelings of hopelessness or feelings of joyous expectation when they commit their fatal act.)

Throughout the 1990s, Americans read and heard of case after case of outbursts by individuals in emotional or psychological crisis that resulted in domestic violence fatalities, drug-related killings, school and workplace killings, and bombings and shootings like those that claimed dozens of lives in Oregon, Oklahoma, Colorado, and other states.[6]

Following each of these cases (particularly the murder-suicides carried out by two white, middle-class teenage boys in April 1999 at Columbine High School), politicians examined policy issues like the question of easy access to firearms and assault weapons while social service and mental health advocates interjected a plea to increase funding for counseling and other mental health services. Missing from these discussions was an appreciation that the mass killings probably stemmed, in part, from the perpetrators' sense of hopelessness mixed with rage. And despite widespread hand-wringing in the aftermath of these lethal incidents, no one seemed able to come up with a reliable formula for identifying early warning signs of the depths of despair and anger that lead individuals to commit such crimes.

Moreover, the glamorization of America's historic culture of violence and its legacy in modern times was not a significant part of the national debate in most circles following the high-profile murder-suicides of the late 1990s. It should have been. The lethal combination of psychological stress, emotional desperation, anger, impulsiveness, and easy access to firearms has characterized the history of American violence from the nation's inception. In that regard, as writer Walter Mosley observes in *Workin' on the Chain Gang: Shaking Off the Dead Hand of History*, blacks in America have been, and continue to be, a petri dish of the nation's psychological health: "The problems experienced by blacks in America have to be seen as part of [a] larger malady.... It is impossible to extricate the black experience in America from the larger American experience."[7]

Only rarely, however, have the negative psychological effects of the nation's history of violence–and the connection between hopelessness and destructive behaviors–been part of the debate about black psychopathologies. Indeed, from European frontiersmen who carried out the two-hundred-year subjugation of Native Americans to white slaveholders who brutalized blacks as a routine, to quick-tempered Southern white "gentlemen" unafraid of drawing their weapons at the hint of a perceived slight, to the evolution of popular entertainment industries that celebrate violent behavior (including nineteenth-century pulp fiction novels that valorized outlaws in the West), America's social fabric has been woven through with violence.

And notably, the relentless glamorization of gangster violence in books, cinema, and television entertainment, which began in the 1920s, has solidified violence within popular culture, making it, by the end of the century, a favorite touchstone for inner-city African-Americans, particularly some self-described hip-hop "gangstas." At the same time, while the public image of crime, violence, and socioeconomic despair in the late twentieth century often took the shape of a young, black or Latino male from the inner city, in reality the face of crime and violence throughout American history has shown a distinctly pale complexion. The contours and shadings of violence have shifted over the centuries, surging or abating with technological advances, demographic changes, and economic trends. But the intensity of violence, like its predominantly white profile, has not waned.

The role of hopelessness in the history of American violence–as distinct from motivations related to racism or quests for power and money–is difficult to appraise. Yet it is likely that hopelessness, especially among lower socioeconomic groups, has contributed to an environment that allowed homicide and suicide rates to escalate during the 1980s and early 1990s. And among African-American youth born after the early 1970s, feelings of hopelessness may be especially painful due to heightened expectations as a result of the civil rights movement. Indeed, though diminished, institutionalized racism, particularly in the employment and economic spheres, has continued. Further, the ascendance during the second half of the twentieth century of advertising-driven commercialism gave rise to an acquisitive ethos in many low-income black communities that led some youths to view material objects such as Nike sneakers and designer fashions as key elements of their identity and self-worth. The gap between desire and the ability to pay for these expensive items may have contributed to a high level of hopelessness-related substance abuse, as well as to black-on-black theft and violence tied to an illegal drug economy.

Although a strong economy during much of the 1990s lessened unemployment among blacks slightly, overall African-Americans experienced an ongoing joblessness crisis during the late twentieth century. The dismal employment figures for blacks in the mid-1990s, for example, were highlighted by Stephen Steinberg in his 1995 look at African-Americans and social policy, *Turning Back:* "In 1994 the unemployment rate was 11.5 percent for blacks and 5.3 percent for whites. According to one estimate, blacks would need 1.6 million jobs to achieve parity with whites."

Furthermore, Steinberg points out, it is an unmistakable conclusion that many of the problems facing the black community can be traced to the high rates of joblessness experienced by blacks, particularly black men: "This job crisis is the single most important factor behind the familiar tangle of problems that beset black communities," Steinberg continued. "Without jobs, nuclear families become unglued or are never formed.... Without jobs, many ghetto youth resort to the drug trade or other illicit ways of making money."[8] Indeed, it is particularly telling that the suicide rate for black males aged fifteen to nineteen more than doubled during this time period, from 3.6 individuals per 100,000 in 1980 to 8.1 per 100,000 in 1996, according to the United States surgeon general.[9]

In *All God's Children: The Bosket Family and the American Tradition of Violence* (1995), journalist Fox Butterfield carefully unearths the link between America's violent past (most notably a destructive impulse born of the Deep South) and its significant impact on Americans today, especially blacks.[10] In telling the story of one black family that has been scarred by violence, despair, and incarceration, Butterfield traces a two-hundred-year-long singularly American thread of violence and follows it to its conclusion: a black man named Willie Bosket, born in 1962, who over thrity years amassed a criminal record ranging from petty theft to a murder that landed him behind bars for life while he was still a young man.

In stunning detail, *All God's Children* recounts the histories of Bosket's father, grandfather, and great-grandfather, all of whom had lengthy criminal records and had spent time in prison. Butterfield's astute analysis shows how the family's ancestral birthplace–a tiny South Carolina county called Edgefield–was virtually founded on violence and mayhem, and how that environment helped shape the Bosket men for generations. What the legacy of Edgefield means in the big picture is chillingly apparent:

> What emerged was not just a portrait of the Boskets, but a new account of the origin and growth of violence in the United States. Violence is not, as many people today presume, a recent problem or a particularly urban bane; and in its inception it had little to do with race or class, with poverty or education, with television or the fractured family–in short, with most of the usual suspects. Rather, it grew out of a proud culture that flourished with the antebellum rural South, a tradition shaped by whites long before it was adopted and recast by some blacks in reaction to their plight. For its adherents, it served almost as a way of life. And at its heart was a lethal impulse.[11]

In exploring the volatile environments of each of the Bosket men, Butterfield illuminates the ways in which violence and despair in the past can all but preordain violence and despair in the future. Sadly, this "lethal impulse" has negatively shaped the experience of many American families. Butterfield's theory that patterns of black violence evolved as "a reaction to their plight,"[12] deserves consideration: any examination of the entirety of United States history shows that African-Americans, like Native Americans, have been the recipients of violence more often than they have been its deliverers. And it seems likely that African-Americans have assumed and continue to act out the violent tradition to a greater degree than whites in response to more than three hundred years of firsthand exposure to it.

American culture, in its romance with violence, has made legends of white gangsters and outlaws such as Jesse James, Bonnie Parker and Clyde Barrow, John Dillinger, and Al Capone. Black gangsters were not romanticized until after the civil rights movement (in movies such as *Superfly* and *Shaft*), but since then, with the rise of rap, they have become cultural icons to whites as well as blacks. (The use of violence to control or overcome feelings of weakness can give individuals a sense of power, particularly if they feel victimized and oppressed. During the black militant era of the 1960s and 1970s, Malcolm X and the Black Panther party argued that for blacks to maintain their own self-respect they needed to strike back with violence in self-defense if they were attacked. And, as discussed earlier, borrowing from Frantz Fanon, many revolutionary-minded blacks felt that violence by the oppressed against oppressors could be psychologically liberating.)[13]

While it is true that many Americans of all races and economic standing receive a consumerist thrill from the "true-life" exploits of criminals, African-Americans, particularly youth who have few positive role models in their communities, are potentially more at risk of suffering negative consequences both personally and as a result of retribution from the larger social system should they adopt the mores of these violent figures. And left unexplored within the national debate about crime in America is the possibility that the nation's violent past combines with pessimistic thinking to produce individuals who live on the brink of psychological breakdown and at the ready to "act out" fantasies of power and revenge with lethal precision.

Additionally, there is a disconnection between the actual consequences of our shared history of violence—namely a culture in which violence pervades across race, class, and educational lines—and the public's perception of modern violence as typically involving black or brown men in urban settings. This collective amnesia results from a general unwillingness to acknowledge the link between oppression, hopelessness, and violence in our history. Seldom is our history of violence discussed in relation to the emotional toll that it has wrought on the black psyche, so it is not surprising that the brief public debate that emerged following the 1990s epidemic of violence by gun-toting white men and boys struck many black Americans as both late in coming and narrowly directed.

Apart from voting to support harsher criminal sentencing laws (particularly for crack cocaine offenses), the building of more jails and prisons, and funding for increased police presence in "crime-prone" neighborhoods, few white political leaders showed much interest in addressing the problems of poverty, violence, and hopelessness that festered in parts of African America during the 1980s and 1990s. In our view, the increase in black suicide and self-destructive behaviors and the crime and violence that have eviscerated vast portions of our African-American communities in the 1980s and 1990s are linked by a steep rise in feelings of hopelessness.

Any serious attempt to explain black suicide must take into account the slippery philosophical and spiritual questions surrounding hope and its attendant impact on mental health and destructive behavior. Research on the question of why some individuals who lose hope—in their future, in their environment, in their relationships—never act out their anger, grief, or frustrations on themselves or on friends or strangers while others do is inconclusive. (For the moment we are leaving aside mental conditions such as bipolar disorder, which involves alternating states of mania and depression, and unipolar disorder, a state of severe clinical depression which may be episodic, that are related to imbalances in brain chemistry and—if correctly diagnosed—can be treated with medication.) And to the layperson, a thorough examination of what causes a loss of hope is too often undertaken only in the aftermath of some extreme manifestation of that loss. Meanwhile, few political and cultural leaders seem capable of finding significant support for marshaling the resources needed to begin identifying and addressing the many societal pressures that contribute to despondency. As we have noted, the state of the black American psyche—particularly the ability to maintain an optimistic outlook about the future and a meaningful role in society—has not been a priority for the nation's health officials.

For many young blacks, particularly those living in deteriorating inner cities and facing few educational or job prospects, the daily grind of merely surviving has left little room for optimism. Of course, thousands of young African-Americans overcome racism and extreme socioeconomic obstacles, as black people have done for centuries, and it is likely that a hopeful outlook and a persevering self-confidence has generated many of their accomplishments: many blacks still live by the motto that every stumbling block must be turned into a steppingstone. But oddly, public discussions of the importance of hope as it relates to emotional and psychological health have not taken place on a consistent, measured basis when black violence and self-destructive behavior are examined. (A witticism offered by the comedian Dick Gregory during the 1960s makes the point about official negligence and cultural denial: "You can't kill yourself by jumping out the basement window.")

For much of their time in America, blacks were optimistic about their chances for better times in the United States, despite the obvious obstacles they faced. The nation was on record as a democratic society, and its legal system and cultural ethos provided the prospect of positive change. A persistent secular hope was typically bolstered by religious faith and the belief that education, hard work, and self-determination would deliver blacks to legal justice and social rewards. During slavery, blacks risked life and limb to keep their families together, better their education, and sustain a degree of personal dignity. Following the Civil War and through the end of Jim Crow segregation in the 1960s, African-Americans saw light at the end of the tunnel as legal challenges were fought against de jure segregation and discrimination. The great Northern migration, the forty-year period during which millions of blacks left the Deep South for Northern and Midwestern cities, was made possible by a robust economy that allowed blacks to make economic gains even as social and legal conditions lagged behind. (Blacks did suffer joblessness during the Great Depression, as did the general population, but the waves of migration out of the South for better job opportunities in industrial centers continued, peaking during World War II.)

By the mid-1950s, crusading black lawyers like Thurgood Marshall had won landmark desegregation cases, particularly the precedent-setting Supreme Court decision of 1954, outlawing segregated schools, which eventually brought an end to legalized discrimination. As a result, a small but solid population of blacks attained middle-class status in many regions of the United States. But still, by the end of the millennium it was necessary to ask a difficult question: For the masses of African-Americans, how did the promises of equality offered during the civil rights movement play out?

For millions of black people, particularly those born after the 1970s, the hope for equitable treatment expressed by their forebears has not been completely realized. While the debate surrounding the reasons for this failure became politicized during the 1990s—with the fight over affirmative action policies being the most visible example—the reality is that about 30 percent of African-Americans are still living below the poverty line and have not benefited sufficiently from the legal, social, and educational opportunities that opened up following the marches, protests, and civil rights actions of the 1960s.[14]

The tendency of white lawmakers and public officials to blame the victims of poverty, however overtly or subtly, has created a social atmosphere in which millions of blacks continue to live in conditions in which the risk of violence and despondency are high. Indeed, by the end of the 1990s, as the U.S. economy experienced an unprecedented period of prosperity, a sense that the nation's poor, homeless, and other marginalized groups were suffering from a character flaw that kept them from becoming rich and suc-

cessful seemed to permeate much of the national consciousness. Stereotypes of black free-loading "welfare queens" abounded, and demands for
welfare reform reached a crescendo. A much-touted but little understood
welfare reform bill was signed into law by President Clinton in 1994. For
African-Americans, this "get tough" attitude has been particularly insidi-
ous. Although some welfare-to-work programs have returned welfare recipients to the workforce, most of these new jobholders still remain at the
bottom of the economy, in low-paying menial and service-sector jobs.

Nor are middle-class black Americans immune from the negative consequences of the belief that blacks and other minorities are solely responsible
for their own "troubles." In January of 2000, at the TransAfrica Forum in
Washington, D.C., the long-term negative influence of white skepticism
about black performance was cited by Georgetown University law professor Mari Matsuda as being a key detriment to the achievement of many
black students: "It is hard for black students not to think that something
must be wrong with them if they find themselves having trouble" adjusting
to life in elite colleges, Matsuda commented. Speaking during a discussion
led by Randall Robinson about the possibility of the U.S. government paying
reparations to blacks for losses they had incurred during and since slavery,
Matsuda said that in her experience the psychological hangover from centuries of social and institutional racism and discrimination reverberates
loudly even within the children of black doctors, lawyers, and other professionals because white society falsely believes that this class of blacks has
"made it."[15] Indeed, for several decades in separate studies, psychologists
have demonstrated how a lack of confidence in their own efficacy has hindered the achievement of black individuals.[16]

Yet in the high rates of black juvenile crime that brought the term "super-
predator" into the vocabulary of lawmakers during the 1980s, in the rise in
pop culture offerings that celebrate teenage "gangsters," and in the hundreds of studies exploring high teen pregnancy and drug abuse rates, we
see abundant evidence that many black hopes and expectations remain un-
fulfilled. While many black and white academics, politicians, and activists,
along with a concerned community of health care professionals, assumed
that the years following the civil rights movement would see masses of
African-Americans improving their quality of life, their assumptions were
only partially correct. At the end of the century, black-on-black crime had
become a greater public health threat for millions; by the mid-1990s, AIDS

was being diagnosed more often among blacks than in the total population; incarceration rates for blacks, particularly black men, have skyrocketed; and income levels for blacks across the board have not risen with the consistency that they have done for whites.

In the Black Power Movement of the 1970s, the pent-up frustrations of many blacks, which had seen its first large-scale voluble expression during the civil rights era, took a newer, more militant and sometimes destructive expression: the urban riots of the 1960s were both an outward manifestation of blacks' loss of hope and an indication that aggressiveness would thereafter be a way of coping with the resulting despair. This despair was heightened when the anti–Vietnam War movement gathered momentum, siphoning off public and private resources from the civil rights movement, effectively slowing the pace of social change for African-Americans. At the same time, the black pride stimulated by the black consciousness movement brought a new self-assurance and assertiveness and a stronger Afrocentric perspective to black Americans that has had a lasting impact.

Nonetheless, the three centuries of black generational anger that had been unleashed by the civil rights and Black Power movements was not directed only at whites. Neither was it free-floating. In a deeply complex manner it metastasized within African America and eventually threatened the general population, primarily in the form of drug-related crime and violence. The absence of reliable and effective institutional initiatives designed to assist blacks in acclimating to post–civil rights era America–including measures to ensure economic opportunity and jobs, affordable and culturally aware health care systems, and community- and school-based programs aimed at promoting healthy self-esteem–left millions of blacks out in the cold, psychologically as well as socioeconomically.

Moreover, the American curse of historic memory loss (abetted by inadequate history curriculums impairing both blacks and whites), has meant that millions of young black Americans who might draw hope from their ancestors' achievements often do not regard the past as a realistic source of inspiration. Compounding the lack of positive role models was the mass movement, after the end of official segregation, of members of the black middle-class to the suburbs, leaving the inner-city population bereft of examples of black success. Schoolteachers, doctors, lawyers, and others with education, training, and stable, well-paying jobs seldom lived side-by-side in the same neighborhoods with the black poor.

Consequently, in many respects the social winds of the 1990s provided little impetus for young black have-nots to believe that their hope (however faint) for a bright future in America would be justified. Even the sons and daughters of black professionals, those African-Americans who attend top schools and obtain well-paying jobs after finishing college are not generally inspired by a firsthand understanding of the optimism and determination that marked the efforts of blacks during the civil rights movement.

These days it is not unusual for young African-Americans to speak of Martin Luther King Jr. and other civil rights leaders in terms that betray their distance from the goals, methods, and achievements of King and his contemporaries. When the hundreds of thousands of African-American men who participated in the Million Man March called by the Nation of Islam gathered at the Mall in Washington, D.C., on October 16, 1995, they represented a milestone in that the generation of blacks born after passage of the Civil Rights Act of 1964 was united with men who well remembered what life was like before the marches of the civil rights era. Yet the emotional momentum that could have been capitalized upon to effectively mobilize young blacks for the new century faded away. The public image of Minister Louis Farrakhan as an antiwhite and anti-Semitic activist, along with the official exclusion of women, deeply divided the black community, precluding a strong, unified initiative. At the same time, whatever one thinks of its social and political stances, the Nation of Islam is not alone among black and white political and cultural organizations in being stumped by the problem of energizing a population (particularly young men) that has been fed more negative signs from society than signs of hope.

Indeed, since during much of the 1980s and 1990s the unemployment rates for black males were routinely the nation's highest,[17] it was not a stretch for many blacks to view the attacks on affirmative action programs and calls for ending welfare programs as thinly veiled assaults on African America, no matter how noble-sounding their proclaimed objectives. In 1992, for example, a national polling firm, Peter D. Hart Research Associates, found that 55 percent of the whites they surveyed believed that "blacks have caused many of their own problems but make excuses by blaming them on discrimination instead."[18] Such attitudes do not bode well for the future of blacks' mental health. In his look at black frustration during the late twentieth century, *Rage of a Privileged Class,* Ellis Cose pinpointed many of the negative implications to be drawn from continued black pessimism. Black parents in the 1990s faced the extremely difficult challenge of guiding their children through a racial landscape for which they have few compasses, Cose argues. And although he stops short of assessing the clinical psychological impact of this kind of pressure, the anecdotal evidence he provides gives solid form to the often amorphous and stealthy quenchers of black hope: "How can [black parents] prepare children for reality's 'rude awakening' while also preparing them for an array of possibilities infinitely grander than those enjoyed by their forebears?" he wrote following interviews with dozens of middle-class black parents struggling to steer their children through the racial morass of America. "How can a parent who came up needing a ton of psychological armor instruct a child who may need only half a ton?"[19] In this statement, Cose was referring to middle-class parents, not poor blacks—who have even greater hurdles to overcome.

The net effect is that millions of blacks, even those firmly established in the middle class, detect in their day-to-day living a brand of residual racism that can be maddeningly subtle yet stubbornly pervasive. Cose's "armor" is part of the burden which blacks carry to protect themselves against mundane racial stresses, even those that are minor. For many young blacks, navigating racial waters that can be deceptively calm becomes, then, a matter of stringing together whatever survival skills are at hand.

Thus, with optimism diminished for millions of blacks following the legal and educational victories of the civil rights movement, traditional coping mechanisms have become less effective: no longer is reliance on the church, extended family, or the larger community of African-Americans a surefire means of ameliorating life's difficulties, particularly those that arise from racism and discrimination, be they internal or external, subtle or not.

When considering the high morbidity and mortality rates among black Americans during the second half of the twentieth century—including those that result from violence and substance abuse—it is likely that hopelessness, in combination with other risk factors such as depression, plays a significant role. Solid research is hard to come by, but in our estimation, a loss of hope and a sense of fatalism among many black Americans is key to explaining the rising rates of suicide, homicide, drug abuse, gun-related violence, and self-destructive behaviors. Indeed, a 1998 study of the influence of religion on the acceptability of suicide among blacks and whites concluded that African-Americans, particularly youth, experienced an increase in suicides during the 1980s and 1990s that the researchers traced to a falling-off of religious beliefs and practices. "Declining levels of religious belief may be associated with loss of traditional protection among African-Americans in particular," the authors wrote in the *Journal of Nervous and Mental Disease*.[20] At the same time, they found that African-Americans "are less accepting of suicide than white Americans. This difference is mainly attributable to higher levels of orthodox religious belief and personal devotion among African-Americans than among white Americans, although emotional, social, and educational differences also play a role."[21] In short, it is likely that blacks, despite a historic rejection of suicide based on Christian indoctrination, are now experiencing a rise in self-destructive behavior that stems from social factors, including economic, educational, and cultural elements.

Therefore, the questions surrounding hope in relation to black mental health are complex and vital. If black Americans endured more than three centuries of epic cruelties under slavery and Jim Crow laws and managed to avoid succumbing to hopelessness and self-destruction in great numbers, why are we seeing a surge in such behaviors now? Was there an element within forced segregation that encouraged blacks to withstand psychological, emotional, and physical hardships in defiance of any suicidal impulses they may have experienced? And, most ominously, are the rising rates of suicides among young blacks, particularly black males, a signal that the mental well-being of the larger African-American population is in danger of collapsing under the weight of new challenges? For instance, will the suicide rate of black women, which has always been low (about 2 per 100,000),[22] begin to rise?

Regrettably, the nation's medical establishment, its political leaders, and the mainstream media have done little to address these questions. And the possibility that some blacks are acting out destructive behavior as a result of long-standing racism-induced self-loathing is not likely to stop whites, or even some middle-class blacks, from voting for politicians who support harsh criminal sentencing laws which disproportionally punish black youth.

The psychological aspects of self-destructive and outwardly directed destructive behavior, and how those behaviors intersect with a loss of hope, tend to enter into public discussion primarily within the context of "personal values." The etherealness of hope and faith make them quicksilver elements amid a churning collection of day-to-day tragedies resulting from crime and poverty. As with the widespread, ill-founded perception that mental illness is a character flaw, an individual experiencing a loss of faith may also fear stigmatization surrounding their agnosticism, adding an extra bit of weight to their already teetering psychic burden. And it is not difficult to imagine that some white Americans (and blacks of middle-class income or socially conservative position) might react negatively to the idea of helping individuals who show no obvious signs of caring about their own lives, families, or communities. Why should we help those who don't care to help themselves? is a typical refrain. Indeed, some family members of mentally ill individuals say that the hardest part of helping a loved one cope with their condition is sustaining a positive outlook.

Usually relatives of suicide victims speak of how the individual "just seemed to give up" in the days or weeks before he or she committed the act. Implicitly, "hope" is what he or she gave up on, and the input and support from friends, family, or clinical mental health workers apparently had little positive influence on the fatal decision. And, as we know, the absence of extended family or professional support for an individual struggling with a loss of hope may also contribute to a rise in destructive behavior. The links between violence, depression, loss of hope, and mental illness exist, but there is no easy way to solve the riddle of how and why a person loses hope or what impact that loss may have on that person's mental health and the carrying out of suicidal thoughts. Yet if one believes, as Amiri Baraka (née LeRoi Jones) wrote in 1966, that "hope is a delicate suffering,"[23] it is possible that the diminishment over several decades of such a life-saving emotion among blacks might occur virtually unnoticed by traditional measurements. To many young black men living in the hurly-burly of today, there is more scorn than pride to be taken from the phrase so loved by civil rights veteran the Reverend Jesse Jackson: "Keep hope alive!" And what some young black Americans have put in the place of traditional hopefulness has not, thus far, proved healthy or effective at insulating them from life-threatening self-destructive behaviors.

Speaking in 1865 on the occasion of the Liberian Independence Day, the black scholar Edward Wilmot Blyden said, "Where there is no future, there is no hope."[24] Blyden could not have foreseen how apt his words would be a hundred years later. But it is obvious that for millions of African-Americans, particularly those at the bottom of the economic ladder, the inability to envision a productive future for themselves has contributed to a devastating loss of optimism.

For many black Americans, suffering has been a familiar condition, and maintaining spiritual and psychological hope was once viewed by many blacks as a worthwhile effort. On the one hand, hope's legacy over the centuries includes much of the labor that built the nation, and magnificent contributions by blacks in the popular and cultural arts, in education and science, in agriculture and the military–in every sector of society. On the other hand, the strength that one derives from holding onto hope even while suffering hardships has been taxed to its limit for too many African-Americans. And all around us are indications that the energy and determination it once took blacks to adhere to hope in the face of a bleak future has been redirected into unhealthy channels.

During the 1980s and 1990s, there were numerous highly publicized stories about blacks in peril and blacks as predators, including the brutal Chicago episode in which two truant school-age boys killed a younger child by dropping him from a high floor of a multistory building in their crime-scarred public housing complex. Their stories were said to be emblematic of life for millions of blacks who haven't entered the middle-class. Tales abounded of "crack mothers" who abandoned their children in filthy apartments, of "gangstas" and cold-hearted "crack slingers," of man-child predators who would just as soon shoot you for your gold necklace as look at you. Unfortunately, the national debate that might have focused on rooting out the causes of such clear symptoms of self-loathing–gun violence, teen pregnancy, alcohol, and drug abuse–instead became a call for more drastic juvenile justice laws, including the practice of trying juvenile offenders as adults so that stiffer penalties can be applied: in 1999, Nathaniel Abraham, a thirteen-year-old black youth who had shot and killed a man when he was eleven, was tried and convicted as an adult in the state of Michigan.[25] This development has ominous implications for the future of many troubled black children who need mental health services much more than they do punitive criminal justice, since jails and prisons place little emphasis on rehabilitation measures. Fortunately, in the case of Nathaniel Abraham, the judge criticized the Michigan law that allows children below the age of fourteen to be tried as adults as basically flawed. Yet the fact that it was enacted at all shows the public's harsh reaction to troubled youth who are desperately in need of a sense of hope.

"Let not the shining thread of hope become so enmeshed in the web of circumstances that we lose sight of it," the black lawyer Charles W. Chestnutt cautioned in 1899.[26] Now, more than a century later, there is a danger that a multitude of circumstances have combined to severely test blacks' willingness and ability to keep hope in sight. This constant straining, this curtailing of faith and hope, has proved harmful to the mental health of millions of African-Americans. Finding solutions to this bleak psychosocial picture will require innovative changes in our institutions and social apparatus. Solving the difficult problems resulting from hopelessness-related violence and self-destruction demands open-minded leadership and a public willingness to acknowledge the importance of well-founded faith and optimism in our collective psychological well-being.

Otherwise it seems quite possible that the same kind of hopelessness-related violence and self-destructive behaviors that have debilitated large parts of the African-American community will provide an epic challenge for the whole nation in the new century.

5

"Stay Strong"

The Legacy of Bearing Up

Whether based in myth or reality, the belief that suicide is "a white thing" has a long history among black Americans. The effect of this belief, and of the perception among both whites and blacks that African-Americans are exceptionally inured to emotional or psychological stresses, has been detrimental. The public's collective understanding of the word "strength" as it is commonly used in relation to blacks–to mean almost superhuman endurance–has in turn made many African-Americans reluctant to seek mental health treatment because of the stigma attached to appearing weak. Furthermore, the Christian faith claimed by most African-Americans has historically upheld the philosophy of "bearing up" at any cost under the pain of slavery and the long-lasting effects of discrimination.

How deeply entrenched are these attitudes at the beginning of the twenty-first century? And what role do they play in creating a social atmosphere in which suicide and many other self-destructive behaviors become possible? In our estimation, these long-held beliefs are woven through the national zeitgeist and are a prevalent if low-key constant of the black American experience. However, they are not completely intractable or invulnerable to positive revision.

To address the various manifestations of these ideas and their impact on the mental health of black people, we must review the ways in which our culture has described African-Americans as at once inferior beings and preternaturally strong.

Consider that today African-Americans are bombarded with a host of cultural and social images in which they are portrayed as physically gifted, as "natural" athletes and entertainers. Simultaneously, they are seen as a downtrodden population inextricably linked to crime and poverty. During the 1990s, for example, blacks, especially males, became nearly synonymous with incarceration and the criminal justice system in America. In 1994, 11.7 percent of black males between the ages of twenty and twenty-nine were incarcerated, according to the D.C.-based Sentencing Project,[1] and by the end of the 1990s, blacks comprised 51 percent of the nation's total prison population. The fact that 52 percent of black inmates were doing time for nonviolent property or drug-related crimes, however, was largely lost on the mainstream media and subsequently on much of the public. At the same time, Americans revered black males who had gained celebrity in public life, such as General Colin Powell, Bill Cosby, and Michael Jordan.

Despite the fact that these are among the nation's heroes, a subgroup of images has formed over the years that reinforce age-old stereotypes of blacks as naturally strong and intellectually and emotionally uncomplicated. The notion that poor black men in particular are somehow "suited" for incarceration is among them.

In 1989, Joel Haycock, in a review article, cited studies of prison suicides that mistakenly concluded that black prisoners were not as inclined to self-injury while in jail as were whites and Hispanics because imprisonment brought a higher degree of pain and stress to the latter two groups than it did to African-Americans. Blacks, it was suggested, were better protected from suicide in prison because their history of hard knocks and "ghetto life" prepared them to withstand the pressures that come with incarceration.[2] In a *New York Times* story in 1982, headlined "Why Are Blacks Less Suicide Prone Than Whites?" a California professor was quoted as maintaining that the black elderly have a lower suicide rate than the white elderly because among blacks "only the strongest survive"; elderly blacks, he argued, feel "a triumph in surviving against adversity."[3]

Undoubtedly, great strength allowed black people to survive slavery and discrimination, but the notion that black men and women can easily handle burdens that would psychologically crush other people has been oversold. The emotional price that they have paid in enduring incredible stresses has too often been dismissed or ignored, and this has hindered the development of mental health services for the black community.

It is important to remember that for any group the perpetuation of stereotypes is not completely external. For example, young male hip-hop artists, when describing their methods of "survival," refer to their need for respect and "props" while they de-emphasize the human qualities that are traditionally feminized—such as empathy and love. The net result is a rigid value system in which men are prized for being "hard" or "strong," and dismissed for being "soft" or "weak." This simplistic image of manhood has been a long time in the making. The exact degree to which blacks may have individually internalized it is difficult to measure and generalizations are risky.

More clear is the presence of low-self esteem and poor self-concept among many African-Americans. Numerous studies of black children, teens, and young adults have shown that racism and discrimination are directly linked to poor self-images among young black Americans. Following the lead of the pioneering black self-image studies conducted by Kenneth and Mamie Clark in the 1940s, psychologist J. K. Morland, for example, found that black children in his 1958 survey routinely, if unconsciously, identified themselves with whites, in large part because "the superior position of whites is emphasized to the Negro children in television, movies, magazines, books and in the pictures on the walls of their nursery schools."[4]

Determining how and why some blacks are able to overcome a negative self-concept resulting from racial oppression and the cultural predomination of whites as the ideal is a question requiring continued research. It is known, though, that a strong, nurturing parent-child relationship is key to protecting a child's self-esteem, especially in a negative environment. But any examination of the level of blacks' internalization of imposed negative images must be accompanied by an acknowledgment that the form and expression of racism can change over time; consequently, blacks' response to race-related stresses, and the effect of those stresses on their self-image, may also vary from era to era. To be sure, one might argue that the changing face of racism in America by the close of the twentieth century—from overt and unmistakable devaluation and even hostility to more subtle and nuanced but still racist attitudes and assumptions—has added a peculiar burden to the black psyche, an element of elusiveness that may compound feelings of isolation and frustration for many African-Americans. In addition, blacks living in poverty (about 30 percent) are much more likely to have low self-esteem and suffer a sense of powerlessness than blacks who have obtained middle-class status or who are more highly educated.

In general, however, the influence of racism on American culture has resulted in a topsy-turvy social construct in which some blacks perpetuate
the damning images that fuel a limited and counterproductive lexicon of
stereotypes about authentic "blackness." And we believe that ultimately
there is a link between blacks' internalization of racist stereotypes, a proliferation of cultural signifiers which reinforce those negative images, and a
rise in self-destructive behaviors, particularly among the poor.

Complicating the psychological aspects of this linkage are social components—such as the reality of black crime and violence among the poor—
that are not easily extricated from our shared cultural experience, and not
easily remedied.

Additionally, the internalization of these images by some blacks may be
tied to a unique set of coping behaviors. Protective factors, such as family
and religion, that may have helped prevent blacks in the past from succumbing to self-destruction should be analyzed with an eye toward assessing their current role in shaping black self-images. Here, separating
myth from reality is crucial. Identifying the exact point where a coping
strategy that once proved effective begins to become destructive is problematic. There is much evidence, however, that historically, blacks who sought
to ameliorate emotional and mental stresses by "self-medicating" with
alcohol and drugs ultimately found that those coping strategies worked
against them by shortening their lives and interfering with education
and employment. The very real reliance on physical strength that blacks
needed to endure centuries of hardship has, in some instances, shifted into
an overreliance on settling problems through physical violence that has
become self-destructive. Moreover, black community protective factors
against suicide, particularly for young men, have weakened during the past
forty years. In particular, the role and influence of the black church and religion in daily life has changed. Therefore, blacks' historic reliance on the
church for spiritual and in many instances secular guidance and security
should also be reevaluated.

Indeed, through the decades, the influence of religion—predominantly
but not exclusively the Christian faith—has added to the widespread notion
that nonmedical resources provided the surest way to assuage emotional or
psychological stress. In many black communities, it is not unusual to hear

individuals facing personal struggles speak of "taking it to the Lord." For many reasons, including lack of access to doctors and fear of official authority, the church traditionally assumed the role of mental health counselor for blacks. And especially for those who have no church, the combination of imposed myths of blacks' "strength" and the distrust that many blacks feel toward the medical and scientific community has produced an isolating environment in which African-Americans across class lines have grown accustomed to suffering in silence.

The predominantly white therapeutic community was rarely looked to by blacks as a viable option for assisting with emotional or psychological stress. In church, however, blacks received a host of messages designed to shore them up under difficult circumstances. It was widely understood that any passing of judgment from the pulpit for indiscretions, including drinking, philandering, domestic violence, or other criminal activity, would not involve the "outside," that is, the white community. And many blacks learned from the church that while drinking, drug abuse, spouse abuse, or criminal activity should be forgiven, suicide is a sin that will keep one's soul from entering the kingdom of heaven. The effect of this indoctrination–and of the church's historic unwillingness to steer troubled adherents toward clinical help–is a potent mixture of fatalism and stoicism. It is vital, therefore, to consider the interplay between the black church's historic presence as a buffer for African-Americans in the midst of a hostile world and its steadfast rejection of suicide as a mortal sin.

In 1992, Kevin Early, a sociology professor at Oakland University in Rochester, Michigan, conducted a rare study of religion and suicide among blacks. After surveying black churches in the Deep South, Early concluded, "From interviews with black pastors . . . we identify an intermingling of religious condemnatory beliefs and secular attitudes about suicide as [an] unthinkable sin, and define it as a 'white thing' alien to the black culture."[5] The hypothesis put forth in numerous studies that the church provided a formidable deterrent against suicide was tested by Early "as a starting point for and basis for future research."[6]

Although Early found that the rejection of suicide by black ministers as a mortal sin was a likely contributor to the relatively low rate of black suicide through the decades, its continuing role as a powerful influence in the larger black community is no longer certain. And, interestingly, Early found that many black ministers draw a solid line between self-destructive

behaviors like drug abuse and drinking, and "outright" suicide: "They do
see a difference between intended suicide as the deliberate and immediate
taking of one's own life, and other actions, such as drug taking. The pastors
obviously do not consider them to be the same thing because they report no
knowledge of suicides or suicide attempts in their congregations, but are
aware of cases of drug and alcohol abuse," Early wrote. "The latter is
viewed as very wrong but an understandable response to the socioeconomic and political condition of blacks in American society, [while] suicide
is defined as unthinkable for black people."[7]

Early's study was valuable, but it stopped short of asking a couple of key
questions: With black ministers failing to acknowledge long-term self-
injurious activities as being a form of suicidal behavior, is it indeed true that
the black church has helped to keep black suicide rates low? Also, if the
black church has been an effective agent for discouraging black suicide,
what happens if increasing numbers of African-Americans move away
from it?

Jewelle Taylor Gibbs, a Berkeley psychologist, surmised that in the late
twentieth century black Americans had experienced a disconnection from
several of the traditional social supports and protective aspects of black culture, including the church, and that this disconnection could be linked to a
rise in many of the pathologies that have been documented among African-
Americans since the post–World War II years.[8] "As the black middle class
has drifted away from the inner cities, it has left a vacuum not only in terms
of leadership but also in terms of values and resources," Taylor Gibbs wrote
in her 1988 book *Young, Black, and Male in America: An Endangered Species*.[9] Arguing that a growing isolation among blacks within class groups
has weakened traditional protective factors, Taylor Gibbs theorized that the
diminished influence of the black church has had several negative consequences. "Many blacks in inner cities no longer seem to feel connected to
each other, responsible for each other, or concerned about each other," Taylor Gibbs wrote. "Rather than a sense of shared community and a common
purpose, which once characterized black neighborhoods, these inner cities
now reflect a sense of hopelessness, alienation, and frustration. . . . It is also
this kind of frustration that erupts into urban crime and violence, family violence, and self-destructive behavior."[10]

While Taylor Gibbs employed a class-oriented model to underscore her
theory of growing black isolation, we believe the crisis in black mental

health crosses educational and economic lines within the black community. Moreover, we would stress that the failure of traditional buffers and protective factors, including the black church, to provide practical and pragmatic answers to the modern problems facing all Americans—including violence, drugs, and potentially fatal sexually transmitted diseases—is exacerbated by a popular culture that elevates some of the negative held-over stereotypes about blacks and "black behavior." And these outmoded perceptions of blacks know no class or educational bounds. (Think of the old racist joke: "What do you call a black man with a Ph.D?" "A nigger!")

It's important that we expand our exploration of how certain stereotypes about blacks came to hold such prominence in popular culture and in the national consciousness—and their impact on the black psyche. This is a huge topic, so we must limit ourselves to highlighting a few examples to make key points.

The image of black people as physically strong and stoically accustomed to difficult circumstances but without higher intellectual sensibilities is woven throughout America's cultural history. As we've noted, this most basic stereotype allowed whites to justify slavery with a minimum of guilt. The perception of blacks as unflinching workhorses is found in songs, spiritual and secular, and in literature by blacks and whites. Much nineteenth-century folklore about blacks—like the story of John Henry, the "steel-driving man" who worked himself to death competing against a machine —was superficially laudatory, but its effects were complex and persistent.

Black athletes, and to a lesser degree, black entertainers, have mostly been characterized by mainstream journalists in terms that highlighted their physical abilities and de-emphasized their intellectual capabilities. A quick survey of key black figures in the sport of boxing provides our first examples. In the early twentieth century, Jack Johnson, the first black world heavyweight champion, was described as a subhuman brute and widely portrayed as a member of a primitive species. In 1997, when former world heavyweight champion Mike Tyson returned to the ring after serving time in prison as a result of a rape conviction, and then twice bit the ear of his opponent, Evander Holyfield, during the bout, his behavior reinforced the image of black men as "savage," and sportswriters employed a range of animalistic imagery to express their outrage and disgust.[11] Speculations were rightly made about Tyson's mental health, and many sportswriters psychoanalyzed the man they had once (somewhat admiringly) dubbed "Iron Mike" without any discernible input from clinical experts, but in 1999, when Tyson went to jail for violating his parole by assaulting a motorist in suburban Washington, D.C., the prospect that he might be receiving mental health counseling during his several weeks of incarceration was scarcely noted.[12]

In the years between Johnson and Tyson, of course, there was a galaxy of black fighters, including Joe Louis and Muhammad Ali, who were valorized by the press and by the public as having awesome physical and instinctual capabilities. In Ali's case, during the early 1960s, when he was a young contender named Cassius Clay, the wit he used to bait opponents and garner publicity was seen as evidence that he might possess a complicated inner life and a healthy intellect only by a few. And his decision to change his name and to publically express political and religious beliefs that did not jibe with the status quo in a turbulent time brought a level of vilification upon him that was breathtaking in its blatant racism. The cumulative effect of such portrayals, even when challenged by some in the media, has been the elevation of blacks—particularly black men—as physically adept individuals whose strength and prowess derive from a primitive source rather than hard work or intellectual gifts.

Over the centuries, a corresponding inner strength was held to be part of blacks' fundamental psychological makeup, a trait that allowed them to "willingly" accept their lower-caste status in society. This, in turn, allowed many whites to believe that blacks lived happily under segregation and in servitude. The image of blacks as either tap-dancing, spoon-playing servants or noble retainers was reinforced by Hollywood films and in popular literature. Thought to be simple-minded and unanalytical, blacks were viewed by many whites as being happy with the merest of life's amenities. Clothes, food, sex, basic shelter, and an occasional holiday feast, along with regular spiritual observance and a good amount of singing and dancing, were widely "understood" to be all that most blacks needed to lead contented lives.

And, as we have noted, an official taxonomy about blacks' physical and mental capabilities, developed by racist white doctors beginning in the eighteenth century, has never quite been laid to rest. As recently as 1994, the widely read book *The Bell Curve,* by Richard Herrnstein and Charles Murray,[13] argued that black Americans on average have a lower IQ than their white counterparts and that this is genetically determined.

The black perspective, however, was markedly different. Blacks during slavery longed for freedom and an opportunity to lead independent lives in which they provided for themselves. Freed blacks following the Civil War wanted nothing so much as an opportunity to work for themselves and to provide homes and services for their own families. Throughout, the "sorrow songs"–the Negro spirituals and gospel hymns that developed from a fusion of African-based rhythms and Christian sacred music and enriched the nation's culture–were artistic manifestations of the struggle to endure dire circumstances. With titles like "Nobody Knows the Troubles I've Seen," and "Deep River, My Home Is Over Jordan," many of these songs evoke both black suffering and the exodus motif which permeates much of black Christian theology. Indeed, the idea that life will be better "on the other side," or in the afterlife (although you couldn't get there through suicide) is a constant leitmotiv of black Christian religion.

The idea that strength is required to endure the difficulties of life on earth has been central to black culture, and psychological, spiritual, and physical endurance enabled African-Americans to withstand more than three hundred years of oppression. But by the early twentieth century signs had surfaced that the degree to which blacks had internalized the limited perception of themselves as preternaturally strong might carry its own dangers. From "sorrow songs" like "Steal Away" to popular songs with titles like "Bad Depression Blues," African-Americans have explored their suffering and canonized their strength and endurance. In a positive sense, black suffering has resulted in some of the most important achievements in American cultural history: Zora Neale Hurston's sad-funny writings of black rural Southern life during the 1920s and 1930s, Langston Hughes's ironic tales of "simple" black men who outwit their white oppressors by feigning ignorance, blues songs like Billie Holiday's "God Bless the Child," and pianist Charlie Spann's "Mississippi Blues" are all examples of African-Americans' abilities to find creative outlets which both expressed and relieved their sorrows and frustrations.

As for the blues, writer James Cone of the Union Theological Seminary in New York referred to blues songs as "secular spirituals." In his 1992 book *The Spirituals and the Blues,* Cone notes that black Christian church leaders did not approve of blues music because it often focused on some of the more unsavory aspects of life–drinking, sex, or depression. But, as Cone explained, "It is not that the blues reject God; rather, they ignore God by embracing the joys and sorrows of life, such as those of a man's relationship with his woman, a woman with her man."[14]

All the same, the overarching message found in much of the spiritual and secular music–and even some poetry and literature–created by blacks over the centuries placed an emphasis on a need for "keeping on" despite incredible psychic and physical difficulties. (The expressions, "I'm going to keep on keeping on" and "Keep the faith" are still popular among black Americans today.) A mid-twentieth century poem by Etheridge Knight, for example, is called "For Black Poets Who Think of Suicide," and contains the lines "Black Poets should live–not leap / From steel bridges, like the white boys do. / Black Poets should live–not lay / Their necks on railroad tracks, like the white boys do. . . . / Let all Black Poets die as trumpets, and be buried in the dust of marching feet."[15]

The legacy of this emphasis has been the entrenchment of a self-image in which African-Americans must be capable of "dealing" with any stress that comes along. Modern versions of this construct have turned toward glamorizing gangs and street life, an evolution which has drawn criticism from some black leaders and from conservative watchdogs who take issue with artists of any color who appear to glorify violence at the expense of more humane qualities. When a black rapper refers to himself as "keeping it real," he is most likely evoking a level of strength, resourcefulness, and reverence for "the 'hood" that he views as an important part of his image. Motion pictures, as a primary tributary of popular imagery, have also contributed to this particular stereotype. Since the 1970s, black Americans have often been portrayed by writers and filmmakers as trash-talking "bad-asses," often physically imposing, quick-tempered individuals, as in blaxploitation films like *Superfly* and *Shaft*.

The landmark late-1970s network television mini-series version of writer Alex Haley's semi-biographical exploration of black history, *Roots,* was an exception to this trend. It was wildly popular and brought–temporarily, as it turned out–the lingering ghosts of slavery onto the front burner of public consciousness. This era was also noteworthy for a handful of "serious" black-oriented films like *Sounder* and *Lady Sings the Blues,* which received critical and popular success. But by the early 1980s, changing market forces, and a lack of black writers and directors powerful enough to push through nonexploitative films about African-Americans, allowed the film industry to revert to damaging portrayals of blacks. Director Spike Lee emerged in 1986 as a prolific and talented filmmaker; whatever the social and artistic merits or shortcomings of his work, in our view what matters most is the fact that he has been, to a large degree, a lone black voice in the Hollywood wilderness.

Other popular black-oriented Hollywood films that were heavily attended by blacks in the 1980s and early 1990s again focused on the strife-torn low-income black experience, including *Boyz N the Hood* (its young black director, John Singleton, did bring some meaningful nuances of urban life to the screen, but these were lost amid the gunplay and drug use that dominated the film), *New Jack City,* and *Juice.* However, Singleton's film *Rosewood* (1998), based on a true story of the massacre of blacks by white racists in a Florida town, did not attract either whites or blacks and quickly failed at the box office. And, in 1999, when talk show titan Oprah Winfrey attempted to explore the traumatic psychological effects of racism in a film version of Toni Morrison's Pulitzer Prize–winning novel *Beloved,* she was also rebuffed by both audiences. "Why can't we put slavery behind us once and for all?" some whites asked following the film's release. "I'm not responsible for slavery, and anyway, I see a lot of black people who are doing pretty good these days." Blacks, too, stayed away from the picture, complaining that Winfrey's portrayal of Morrison's Sethe—a runaway slave who kills her child rather than let her be taken by slavers—was too grim. "Why do we have to go there again?" some blacks questioned. And, troublingly, the significant amount of personal and professional strength Winfrey displayed in mounting this difficult film did not seem to inspire admiration among many African-Americans.

On the small screen, a fuller range of black life has emerged, but it still represents a drop in the ever-expanding bucket of popular entertainment. In the 1970s, white liberal producers like Norman Lear attempted to bring realistic portrayals of "black life" to network television with shows like *Good Times* and *The Jeffersons.* During the 1980s, *The Cosby Show* (for which coauthor Alvin Poussaint served as a production consultant) offered a truer glimpse at upper-middle-class black life that belied the nouveau riche antics of George and Louise Jefferson and became one of the most popular network sitcoms of the decade. But by the 1990s, African-Americans could be found most often on the three major broadcast networks in the roles of stern police lieutenants in crime dramas or fun-loving sidekicks in situation comedies.

A bevy of black-oriented sitcoms on upstart cable and alternative networks were on the air by 1996, and these became popular choices for black viewers. On the three major networks, however, blacks and Latinos were still woefully absent from starring roles in most of the high-profile prime-time sitcoms. And for some the nature of the virtually all-black comedies airing on the smaller, newer networks like WB and UPN was offensive. Many of these shows featured main characters who were modern versions of the "shuckin' and jivin'" stereotypes of yore; in *Malcolm and Eddie* and on *Martin,* two early 1990s sitcoms that caught on with black viewers, the actors portrayed men who were embarrassingly brash, immature, and self-serving. For young black consumers of televised entertainment in the 1990s, the chances of encountering shows offering thoughtful explorations of black life–and which showed blacks as complicated, multilayered individuals–were slim.

Meanwhile, in popular music some black artists and producers finally gained control over their work beginning in the late 1980s. But for the most part they continued to offer content that did little to correct expectations about blacks, particularly black men, as physically powerful, emotionally immature individuals for whom commanding "respect" at all costs is the ultimate expression of strength. At the same time, black female rappers routinely crafted their images as strong, savvy women who took no guff from any trifling black man, extending a long-standing perception of black women as stoics who struggle to maintain their families without the help of black men.

Overwhelmingly, the continuing emphasis on violence, drug abuse, and sexual conquest in rap and hip-hop music, and in popular films, is part and parcel of the self-image deficiencies that have plagued African-Americans for decades.

The pervasiveness of these images in popular culture–in television, music, and films–has given rise to a romantic notion of urban life that has had a curious impact on society. By the end of the 1990s, in an intriguing cultural transference, white teenagers (often referred to as "wiggers") were wearing "ghetto clothing" like hooded sweatshirts and extra-baggy jeans, and peppering their language with black slang like "nigga" and "gangsta." Apparently the media's distorted version of what constituted "black" behavior, especially the hardened, take-no-prisoners posturing, had a strong appeal for some white youths. The implications of young whites adopting these negative images of "blackness" are debatable, but it is quite possible that these youth, struggling to cope with their own anomie, identified with what they perceived as blacks' strength and creativity.

During the late 1990s, faint signs emerged that some black entertainers were at least aware of the self-destructive thread of violence running through the black community and the role of popular culture in encouraging destructive behavior, including homicide and suicide. One might argue that Tupac Shakur, a young black hip-hop artist who began his career as a poet, was an embodiment of this thread. In interviews he often spoke of being saddened by the violence, drug abuse, and guns that seemed to be part of his life but which he seemed to be unable to avoid. And before his death in 1996—he was killed by a gun-wielding assailant thought to be resentful of his popularity and allegiance to the "West Coast" clique of rappers—Shakur referred to his feelings of hopelessness and isolation in a track that might be seen as representing a *cri du coeur* for many of today's young black males. In a song titled "Lord Knows," Shakur rapped, "I smoke a blunt [a cigar hollowed out and stuffed with marijuana] to take the pain out / And if I wasn't high, probably try and blow my brains out."[16]

By the end of the century, however, Tupac Shakur's short life had become a rallying point for many black hip-hop artists who said that they were fed up with the violence and self-destructive lifestyles they once embraced. It remains to be seen whether their creative output will begin to match their words—or whether the black community will continue to support a form of popular music that rose to prominence on the historic image of the black man as a super-strong individual who needs neither love nor redemption to make his way through life.

6

Blacks and
Victim-Precipitated Homicide

*"Suicide by Cop," Fatalistic Behavior,
and Mental Illness*

The phrase "suicide by cop" was initially used by psychologists and criminologists in the early 1980s and caught the public's attention within the next decade. It describes a confrontation in which an individual arms himself, enters a public space, and appears to goad law enforcement officials into shooting him. It was reportedly coined by a former California police officer, Karl Harris, who worked for a suicide prevention center after leaving law enforcement. In an interview with the *New York Times* on June 21, 1998, Harris said that he'd encountered this type of suicide both as a police officer and later in talking with callers to the suicide hotline. "As a cop, I knew of a number of cases where it appeared that people had actually forced police officers to shoot them," Harris told the *Times*. And, he continued, while manning the hotline, "I saw all the different ways people attempted suicide and it occurred to me that maybe some people were actually forcing cops to shoot them because they wanted to die."[1]

By the end of the 1990s, suicide by cop seemed to represent a volatile new eruption of the combustible formula of guns plus mental illness. The idea that police officers–who work extremely difficult jobs under a high degree of public scrutiny–might be forced to shoot someone to death as a result of that person's suicidal behavior resonated within the public imagination.

But suicide by cop is not as simple as it may appear from the limited media coverage it has received. And even as it has come to be defined foremost in a law enforcement context, it is merely the latest wrinkle in a psychosocial phenomena that is little known outside clinical circles: suicide by means of victim-precipitated homicide. First used in 1959 by criminologist Marvin E. Wolfgang, "victim-precipitated homicide" is a concept that is laden with the ambiguities of human psychology and behavior, as well as the elusive nature of mental illness.[2] Ultimately, both suicide by cop, and the broader category of victim-precipitated homicide are not as clear-cut as they appear at first blush.

While the shocking image of a police officer made to kill a presumably suicidal person holds a somewhat dramatic place in the public consciousness, we believe the theory warrants careful examination before law enforcement agencies can claim it, unchallenged, as a viable explanation for any lethal shooting. Further, we believe that in instances where an individual is obviously mentally ill and posing a weapons-related threat to the public and law enforcement officers, police agencies should direct their resources to disarming the person through nonlethal means. The fact that the gun-wielding individual may say words or leave a note indicating his desire to die at the hands of authorities (which has occurred), should not preclude police from devoting all available resources to neutralizing that person without killing him. Indeed, even in the worst-case scenario–such as an armed individual who clearly aims his weapon at officers and utters words indicating his wish to die–could not the officers shoot to disable without releasing a deadly barrage?

A July 1999 Fort Lauderdale incident illustrates the potential problems with accepting at face value the suicide by cop theory. In this case, a twenty-two-year-old mentally disturbed black man walked down a busy street in a predominantly African-American neighborhood carrying a pistol. Jimmy Thompson was known as a mentally "slow" but essentially harmless person around the working-class neighborhood where he lived. On this stifling midsummer afternoon, Thompson crossed one side of Sistrunk Boulevard, stood on the median, and began pacing back and forth as cars zipped by. After a crowd gathered, some witnesses who knew him urged him to drop the gun and get off the median.

When members of the Fort Lauderdale police department arrived a short time later they found Thompson marching about waving the pistol. After spending thirty-two minutes attempting to convince him to drop the gun, three of the two dozen officers on the scene opened fire. The officers who fired, none of whom were African-American, said later that they pulled their triggers because Thompson appeared to be moving his gun in a "threatening" manner. The man was hit by several bullets and died two days later in a Broward County hospital.[3]

After they shot Thompson, the police learned what many of the black witnesses to the ordeal had suspected: the gun was not loaded. On the surface, the police argument for firing at him was legitimate. The officers said they had no way of knowing that the gun was unloaded and they could only assume that Thompson was endangering innocent bystanders and public safety officers at the scene.

According to a witness who was later quoted in the *Miami Herald*, Thompson had said the words, "Just kill me" during the standoff (although an audio-free videotape of the last fifteen minutes of the incident made by a black citizen who lived nearby did not show Thompson mouthing those words).[4] According to a city council member and a reporter from the *Herald*'s Broward County staff who viewed the tape, the video does show Thompson pacing the concrete median, alternately pointing the gun toward his waist and toward his head and waving it around. Neighborhood bystanders, including one who identified herself as a friend of Thompson's, said that he had been talking about killing himself in the hours before. Other locals said they believed that he was drunk and looking for attention (relatives later confirmed that Thompson had been drinking earlier in the day).[5] In the midst of the thirty-two-minute standoff, Thompson's mother, Cassandra, who lived near the scene, was visited by Fort Lauderdale police officers, but they would not let her speak with her son. At the time, the officers believed that Thompson might have become further agitated by his mother's presence at the scene.

In the aftermath of the shooting, the police chief defended the officers who'd killed Thompson. "It did take thirty minutes before we fired—but the time is dictated entirely by the circumstance," Michael Brasfield said to the *Herald*. "When a man is barricaded in his home, in a controlled environment, we've been known to wait days before acting. But in a public setting the rules are different."[6]

For Cassandra Thompson—who said her son was mentally disturbed and would not take his medication—his death was a gross miscarriage of justice. She did not disclose the precise nature of his mental illness nor the kind of medication he was supposed to be taking; all the same, she said, "He needed to be talked to, not shot at." The shooting precipitated a hastily called meeting in a community center near Sistrunk Boulevard, attended by many black residents who were upset by the incident.

"It was very sad," said Carlton Moore, a black Fort Lauderdale City Council member who represents the district where the shooting happened. "When I watched that videotape, I found myself torn—part of me doesn't think the cops handled it well, that they could have done something other than kill him," said Moore during an interview five months after the shooting. "But part of me knows that if I were in their shoes, it would have been a tough call because they didn't know that the gun wasn't loaded."[7]

Such incidences, usually played for drama in superficial news stories, have a powerful influence on the public's perception of how law enforcement agencies handle mentally disturbed individuals who appear threatening. They also negatively influence the public perception of how blacks are treated should they engage law enforcement officers during a moment of psychological distress. It is understandable that the randomness of violent acts committed by individuals suffering from mental illness is especially frightening to the public and to law enforcement officials. But the fact that most Americans will never be the victim of such an unprovoked attack is not usually incorporated into media coverage.

At the same time, there is little disagreement that the numbers of severely mentally disturbed people living on the streets of our nation's cities has increased during the past twenty years. For several decades many severely mentally ill people nationwide have been "deinstitutionalized"—discharged from state mental hospitals to community resources that are inadequate; many have become homeless. And without a radically improved multi-agency effort designed to humanely identify, treat, and rehabilitate mentally disturbed people who are on the street, random acts of violence by individuals experiencing psychological distress will continue to occur.

The combination of public fear and a woeful lack of political leadership has left many jurisdictions, including city officials and law enforcement agencies, pretty much on their own with regard to establishing humane policies for coping with severely mentally ill street people. In November 1999, for example, following several random attacks on citizens by mentally disturbed men in New York City, Mayor Rudolph Giuliani announced plans to arrest street people who refused to avail themselves of city-run homeless shelters. Saying that he sought to protect the majority of the city's residents from individuals who might be mentally ill and potentially dangerous, Giuliani planned to limit the civil liberties of some of New York's most helpless residents.[8]

Amid the heated public and political debate that followed Giuliani's announcement, the difficulties inherent in treating mentally ill homeless people were highlighted by social services advocates but scarcely acknowledged by law enforcement officials or the mayor. That same month New York governor George Pataki announced plans to allocate $125 million to mental health programs in the state. Of course, that decision had been arrived at only after Pataki came under harsh criticism for signing previous budgets that underfunded mental health programs, and after two highly publicized assaults by mentally disturbed homeless men on strangers had shocked and outraged New Yorkers. Mental health and homeless advocates welcomed the additional resources—the $125 million would supplement the $4.2 billion that New York spends annually on mental health services—but they also pointed out that the state's longstanding practice of deinstitutionalization has resulted in a shortage of beds and supervised housing units that will likely take many more years and many millions of dollars more to correct.

At the same time, Pataki and Giuliani are not alone among elected officials who are desperate to neutralize the negative impact of millions of undertreated mentally ill people living on our nation's streets. Nor are they alone among politicians in failing to make mental health a priority issue, to summon the moral and political will that is required to adequately fund mental health services. Indeed, by the time Democratic Vice President Al Gore and his wife, Tipper, sponsored a mental health conference in the late summer of 1999, mayors in New York, San Francisco, and several other cities were testing the Constitution in drastic attempts to control the homeless populations in their towns—ticketing those who lay on sidewalks, taking away their shopping carts, and confiscating personal belongings.

In a larger sense, the collective influence of culture, racial discrimination, psychology, and history on human behavior is usually ignored when trying to understand why some mentally disturbed individuals attack strangers. People respond out of fear, and even in attacks in suicide-by-cop killings, the presence of a unique sociological alchemy is not likely to be considered. The general perception of "dangerous" mentally ill people held by much of the public is limited and unenlightened, in part because media coverage emphasizes the drama and tension of these confrontations between authorities and mentally disturbed individuals and overlooks the possible strategies for nonlethal resolutions, including various forms of physical restraints. And with the exception of a December 1999 declaration by U.S. Surgeon General David Satcher that millions of Americans are struggling with mental illness and finding few affordable resources, the nation's political community and medical establishment have not provided positive leadership on this front.

By taking the law enforcement position at face value—that the only recourse is to kill an armed mentally disturbed individual in order to forstall the loss of innocent lives—news organizations and the public are sacrificing due process and eroding the once-sacred tenant that every human life is worth saving. And when a racial gap exists between law enforcement officials and the citizens they are sworn to protect (in most large urban centers, the majority of officers patrolling the streets and investigating crimes are white and or live in the suburbs, while the residents in their work areas are likely to be black or Latino) you have a recipe for disaster.

Consider that many black men, whether they are homeless, mentally disturbed, or upwardly mobile college graduates, view encounters with the law as potentially life-threatening. For them, the possibility that a police officer, particularly a white officer, might beat, choke, or shoot a black man with little or no provocation is an ever-present reality. From the notorious cases of Deep South police officers killing and wounding dozens of black men before and during the civil rights movement to the numerous controversial incidents of police officers beating and shooting blacks in every region of the country in the 1990s, stories of black men abused by law enforcement officials had by the end of the twentieth century taken on an apocalyptic tone. And many African-American men continue to believe that a split-second wrong move with a law enforcement officer—especially a white officer—could bring about their death or serious injury.

Additionally, the combination of some blacks' reluctance to admit mental distress out of fear of appearing "weak" or "crazy" and a machismo code of the street that emphasizes physical confrontation over verbal negotiation creates an environment in which a black man in severe emotional distress might view dying by a police officer's bullet as an "honorable" way to go. In 1986, *Essence* magazine published portions of a letter written by a twenty-three-year-old black man which illustrates the depth of shame experienced by many who consider self-murder–and the depths of despair and self-loathing that nonetheless drives hundreds of young African-American men to end their own lives: "Mom, don't tell anybody I killed myself. Just tell them somebody killed me because I don't want people to think I'm crazy.... Please don't take this too hard because it's the only way out for me. Take care of yourself and try not to lose any sleep over this." The young man, who later put a gun to his temple and killed himself, also wrote, "This is a very cold world and I just wasn't ready for it."[9] In some cases, distraught young black men want to put themselves in situations where the odds are great that they will die at the hands of others.

Comprehensive studies of the phenomenon are few, and none have yet been nationwide, but a December 1998 paper on suicide by cop published in the *Annals of Emergency Medicine* provided what is perhaps the most complete look at this issue. Conducted in greater Los Angeles by researchers from Harvard Medical School and the Los Angeles area, the study suggested that "all officer-involved shootings should be examined to determine whether they are actually a law enforcement-forced-assisted suicide, and deaths related to this phenomenon should be recorded as suicide by coroners and medical examiners."[10] The researchers arrived at this conclusion after examining 46 instances of suicide by cop in the Los Angeles region between 1987 and 1997. Of these, only 5 involved blacks (which reflects the demographics of the area), but the study is nevertheless relevant to our inquiry.

These 46 incidents were among 437 officer-involved shootings examined by researchers, with the largest number, 13, occurring in 1997. The ages of the suicidal individuals ranged from eighteen to fifty-four, and during the decade in question only one woman had been involved in a suicide-by-cop confrontation. In the majority of the cases studied, 65 percent, researchers found that the individuals showed "suicidal intent" through verbal communication to family members or friends, while 43 percent of the cases involved individuals who "exhibited suicidal characteristics or behavior."[11] In 10 of the cases (21 percent), the individuals used "verbal communication" with officers to express suicidal thoughts. And "in all 46 suicide by cop cases, there was evidence that suicidal individuals specifically wanted law enforcement officers to shoot them." Additionally, all 46 of the individuals "displayed a lethal weapon or what appeared to be a lethal weapon during the confrontation with law enforcement officers," with 22 of the cases involving guns.[12]

Many confrontations, 23, took place at the individual's private residence, and 13 occurred "at large in the community." In 7 cases, the individuals actually fired at the police. In total, 25 of the individuals died after being shot by the officers. (The study also found that those who died were classified by the coroners in their respective jurisdictions as homicides, not suicides, an across-the-board practice that must be reexamined before public safety and health officials can begin to grasp the causes and potential solutions of this phenomenon).[13]

Among the characteristics of the individuals killed in these confrontations are several telling details: 32 percent had prior arrest records, 30 percent had histories of drug or alcohol abuse, 18 percent had been involved in domestic violence disputes, and 29 percent had histories of psychiatric treatment.[14] Given these numbers, it is likely that drug abuse, domestic violence, mental illness, or previous contact with law enforcement agencies played a role in many of these incidents. Yet without further detailed information about the precise nature of each case, it is difficult to determine how large a role mental illness, strictly defined, played in precipitating any of these showdowns with police.

Beyond suicide by cop there are other instances in which individuals place themselves in harm's way with full knowledge that they may be killed. Although the official clinical definitions of suicidal behavior do not fully encompass all of these actions, particularly where young black males are concerned, perhaps they should. Few comprehensive studies of blacks and victim-precipitated homicide exist, but some researchers have included this broader concept in their examinations of blacks and suicide. Berkeley psychologist Jewelle Taylor Gibbs, for example, in a 1997 paper entitled "African-American Suicide: A Cultural Paradox," writes: "Black males, responding to feelings of anger and alienation, sometimes engage in violent confrontations with the police, family or peers, resulting in victim-precipitated homicide, arguably a form of extreme suicidal behavior."[15] Moreover, Taylor Gibbs notes, other factors such as access to guns and impulsivity also play an important part in victim-precipitated homicides among blacks: "The easy availability of guns in the inner city is a significant factor in the rising rates of suicide and homicide of black youth and adults, many of whom are chronically frustrated and often impulsively direct their aggression against themselves, as well as others."[16]

For people of any race, the precise meeting point of aggressive behavior, homicide, and suicide can be difficult to identify. For example, an individual who fears his wife or girlfriend is leaving him, and threatens to kill her and then himself, may be identified as suicidal and homicidal. On the other hand, an individual who kills his wife or girlfriend and then turns the gun on himself may be acting impulsively without previous suicidal thoughts. He may prefer to kill himself than be captured and serve a lifetime in jail or face the death penalty. The final outcome, of course, is still self-inflicted death, but there is no guarantee that the latter scenario will bear the hallmarks of what is traditionally considered suicidal behavior. (Although because of the severe grief they may invoke, stressful domestic situations, including romantic breakups, are usually included among primary suicide risk factors.)

Culture and social class also play a role. Among inner-city blacks and Latinos, in particular, some young men, when interviewed by law enforcement or mental health workers following a violent confrontation, have said that they "didn't care" if they died during the incident. When asked whether they knew their actions had put their lives at risk, some have answered in the affirmative but also allowed that they "had to do what they had to do," often because they had been "dissed" (disrespected). This bravado posture is complicated and may not immediately register as suicidal with social workers or police unschooled in the nuances of street culture.

The combination of racial history, cultural identity, and self-image can be a formidable veil for clinical practitioners, social workers, and law enforcement officials to penetrate. For some young black men, protecting their honor on the street, safeguarding their reputation as "hard," or as a "gangsta" or a "playa," is an ongoing process that might at some point involve putting one's life on the line. On the street, this willingness to take life-threatening risks might be viewed as a form of dueling that the participants see as a necessary part of their survival. Harvard theologian and philosopher Cornel West refers to this kind of behavior as violence borne of "despair and nihilism."[17] Indeed, the prospect that nihilism—expressed within the black community as a reaction to the emotional pain of family and community breakdown–fuels the self-destructive behavior exhibited by some blacks is a subject deserving much more extensive research.

The 1998 case of a black man in Kentucky provides a chilling glimpse into the unexplored links between race, mental illness, and victim-precipitated homicide. In late February, Bob Jones, a black man with a history of erratic behavior, and his wife, the acclaimed novelist Gayl Jones, barricaded themselves in their home in a quiet Lexington neighborhood. Jones was wanted by police for allegedly making threats against local hospital administrators and law enforcement officials, threats in which he accused them of having killed his mother-in-law after she went to the University of Kentucky Markey Cancer Center for treatment.

After a three-hour standoff, police stormed into the house on Locust Avenue, fearing that Bob and Gayl Jones would carry out threats they had made to blow up the house by igniting the gas they'd turned on. At the very instant that members of a special police unit trained to serve warrants on the mentally ill broke down the door, Bob Jones cut his own throat with a knife. He bled to death; his wife was taken to a local hospital for observation. The sad story of Bob and Gayl Jones made the headlines primarily because of the professional standing of Gayl Jones–and reports emphasized the apparently tragic turn her life had taken.

But Bob Jones (who had used several aliases during his twenty-year odyssey from his origins in a small Michigan town, where he'd first gotten into trouble with police after protesting at a gay rights rally, to his bizarre actions in Lexington in 1998) demonstrated symptoms of a mental illness that is often expressed through extreme racism and paranoia. And while it is likely that he may have suffered from a chemical imbalance–schizophrenia or manic depression–his behavior evinced an especially volatile form of paranoia.

The breakdown of mentally ill individuals who had not received adequate treatment, or who spurned treatment because their illness convinced them that they didn't need help, led to other explosive encounters between law enforcement officers and armed individuals in the 1990s, including several cases where white men shot or killed members of minority communities, including Jews, because they believed those ethnic groups were "taking over" the country.[18] Individuals who commit such hate crimes are not officially classified as mentally disturbed by the American Psychiatric Association, creating a puzzling deficiency in our culturally shaped system of psychiatric classification.

In this connection, we recognize that Americans are loath to label even extreme racist behavior as a form or symptom of mental illness. In the early 1990s, for example, a mentally disturbed black man named Colin Ferguson shot and killed several passengers on a commuter train in New York. After being deemed fit to stand trial, Ferguson won the right to defend himself, resulting in one of the most bizarre criminal proceedings in modern history. Having fired his court-appointed counselors in part because they wanted to employ a defense built around the questionable state of his mental health, Ferguson—who had rambled incoherently and shown signs of being delusional on the day of the shootings and when he was arrested—set about defending himself in court. Throughout the weeks-long trial proceeding, which was broadcast on cable television, Ferguson was by turns overwrought, unresponsive, and generally out of touch with reality as he insisted that someone else had killed the passengers. As eyewitness after eyewitness took the stand to rebut Ferguson's version of events, he consistently referred to himself in the third person and continued to insist that someone else had fired numerous rounds into the crowded railcar.

The fact that Ferguson had shot only white people—and that he had spoken to acquaintances and family members prior to the killings about hating white people—led some to dub his a case of "black rage." (Indeed, the defense attorneys had discussed using a "black rage" defense before Ferguson took over his own case.) After he was found guilty of several murders and sentenced to multiple life sentences, some of the jurors said they found it obvious that he was mentally ill, regardless of the racial component that may have been involved in his deadly actions. And although Ferguson's illness was on public display in all its sad confusion, the net effect of the media coverage of his trial was to reinforce the old stereotype of a menacing black man who is willing to take up arms and kill white people.

Then there is the case of Buford Furrow Jr., a white man who admitted to going on a hate rampage in Los Angeles in 1999, several months after he had been evaluated by the Washington State mental health system. On a hot morning in the late summer of 1999, Furrow shot up a Jewish community center, wounding several workers and one child, then fled into the surrounding residential neighborhood, where he allegedly killed a Filipino postal worker. Furrow belonged to a neo-Nazi group that was anti-Semitic and against all people of color, and the shootings were reported as racially motivated hate crimes.

The possibility that individuals holding extreme racist beliefs may suffer from a form of mental illness is controversial within the psychiatric community. In the wake of the Furrow shooting, Renee Binder, the chairwoman of the American Psychiatric Association's Council on Psychiatry and Law, said that racism "is not something that is designated as an illness that can be treated by mental health professionals."[19]

The American Psychiatric Association (APA) has never officially recognized racism as a mental health problem, for perpetrators or victims, although the issue was raised more than thirty years ago. After multiple racist killings during the civil rights movement, a group of black psychiatrists sought to have murderous bigotry based on race classified as a mental disorder. The APA's officials rejected that recommendation, arguing that since so many Americans are racist, racism in this country is normative—a cultural problem rather than an indication of personal pathology. In addition, the Association said, calling racism a mental illness might appear to absolve racists of their moral and legal responsibility, thus decreasing their motivation for self-examination and rehabilitation, and limiting the judicial options for prosecutors should these individuals act on their beliefs in violation of the law. The group also suggested that racists do not show symptoms that are distinctive enough to fit any of its diagnostic categories.[20]

We believe that this position is ill-founded. Extreme racism is a serious mental illness. A person who believes that any group of "others" is responsible for the world's troubles—and must be eliminated—meets criteria for a paranoid "delusional disorder," a major psychiatric illness included in the *Diagnostic and Statistical Manual of Mental Disorders*, an index of mental illnesses published by the APA that influences legal rulings, legislation, and public policy. For individuals, criteria for a delusional disorder include experiencing non-bizarre delusions (false beliefs that cannot be changed by presenting correct opposing evidence) that last at least one month. Many delusional persons exhibit serious social dysfunction. The average person may be reluctant to consider racially motivated attacks as symptoms of mental illness because they don't truly understand the complexities of mental illness. But, as it is well within the APA's power to improve the public's awareness of how racism contributes to and may be a part of some forms of mental illness, it is vital that the organization provide progressive leadership on this admittedly unpopular but vastly important issue.

Human behavior, after all, occurs on a continuum; insanity is not always immediately obvious. Psychotic people with delusional disorders often function so well that they aren't seen as seriously disturbed, even by experts who evaluate them. Such people are very sick nonetheless. Like all others who experience delusions, extreme racists do not think rationally. Instead, they create fantastical theories about who is responsible for their problems, a symptom of their crippling paranoia which requires intervention. Untreated, such individuals may act out homicidal and suicidal rage.

Among blacks, depression and symptoms of posttraumatic stress syndrome resulting from regular exposure to violence may also constitute a mental illness that neither they nor clinicians would readily recognize or acknowledge. And it is not far-fetched to argue that many of the pathologies currently bedeviling much of the black community—including high rates of drug and alcohol abuse, health-threatening diets, and violence—are fatalistic life-threatening behaviors that can be viewed as long-term or slow-motion suicide. Individuals experiencing poor health due to overeating, alcohol abuse, or drug abuse often go unchallenged by relatives if they keep up the appearance of "normalcy": holding down a job or at least keeping their addiction under wraps. The fact that African-Americans suffer from cirrhosis of the liver, heart ailments, sexually transmitted diseases, and obesity-related illnesses in disproportionately higher numbers than whites may be evidence that some African-Americans turn to food, drugs, alcohol, or even sexual activity as a form of medication to ameliorate stresses resulting from racism, discrimination, and other social pressures. These behaviors, however, are only lately being considered by mental health researchers as sometimes falling under the general category of "suicidal" (of course, education, access to medical care, and cultural traditions also play a role).

In the meantime, public awareness of the link between homicide and suicide is limited. To the layperson, reports of violent crimes by mentally disturbed individuals, of suicides by cop, and of the high-profile murder-suicides that gripped the nation during the late 1990s all blur together. The social context provided by the few serious scientific or sociological studies of victim-precipitated homicides or fatalistic behaviors that result in slow-motion suicide is not generally appreciated. More studies must be undertaken, by government and private institutions, in order to effectively address the problem of individuals, black and white, who put themselves and others in harm's way during times of mental distress.

Surgeon General Satcher noted in 1999 that hopelessness and isolation—two risk factors that are present in most suicides—may be a primary contributing factor for the high rates of homicide in the black community.[21] But accurately gauging the level of isolation and hopelessness that tips the scales toward self-destruction is difficult. Until more is understood about the elusive psychodynamics underlying victim-precipitated homicide, suicide by cop, and fatalistic life-threatening behavior, law enforcement officers, public health officials, and policymakers should adopt a compassionate stance when establishing practices for managing mentally distressed individuals in potentially deadly situations.

7

"He Went Out Like a Man";
"She Was a Strong Sistah"

*Questions about the Suicide Gap
among Black Men and Women*

During the 1930s, a Roosevelt administration initiative, the Federal
Writers' Project, sent historians and research assistants into the Deep
South on a mission to record the words and memories of former slaves.
Many of these graphic stories, which are now in the Library of Congress,
made their way into published accounts. One of them, a 1945 book called
Lay My Burden Down: A Folk History of Slavery, includes the recollections
of an African-American woman named Ida Blackshear Hutchinson, the
daughter of slaves.

Born in Arkansas in 1865, Ida Blackshear Hutchinson was seventy-three
years old when she told a Writers' Project researcher of a story she had first
heard during Reconstruction. The editor of *Lay My Burden Down,* B. A.
Botkin, titled Hutchinson's recollection "They Didn't Get Lucy or Her
Quarter":

> They say Negroes won't commit suicide, but Isom told us of a girl that
> committed suicide. There was a girl named Lu who used to run off
> and go to the dances. The patrollers would try to catch her but they
> couldn't because she was too fast on her feet. One day they got after her
> in the daytime. . . . She ran to the cabin and got her quarter which she

had hid. She put the quarter in her mouth. The white folks didn't allow the slaves to handle no money. The quarter got stuck in her throat and she went on down to the slough and drowned herself rather than let them beat her and mark her up. . . . They didn't let the patrollers come on the Blackshear place, but this gal was so hard-headed 'bout going out that they made a 'ception to her. And they intended to make her an example to the rest of the slaves. But they didn't get Lucy.[1]

While it is impossible to know with certainty what black suicide rates were in the nineteenth century, this oral history helps us understand that suicide did occur among African-Americans during their early years in the United States. Two hundred years later, numerous unanswered questions remain surrounding the nature of suicide in general, and about black suicide in particular. And while we can probably draw some conclusions from Lucy's suicide, including the likelihood that she had given up hope (fatalism), it is impossible to know if key risk factors that we currently associate with suicide were present in her case—depression, impulsiveness, mental illness, or anger.

More than merely a poignant folktale, the story of Lucy raises a specific set of gender-related questions that continue to intrigue researchers of African-American suicide: Do black men and women differ in the way they respond to psychological stress? Are there differences in the way that black men and black women respond to racial oppression and discrimination? Are there differences between the coping skills used by black men and those used by black women? The answers to these questions may provide additional clues about the cultural factors that have contributed to a rise in black male suicide in modern times.

Despite the lack of reliable research on black psychology dating back to slave times, it is important to consider whether the socioeconomic standing of black men and black women has, historically, had any bearing on black mental health and suicide. Is it possible, for example, that the sharp increase in suicides among black males in their twenties that began in the 1980s is due, at least in part, to social and economic events? Considering what we know of national employment trends during the twentieth century, is it possible that the emerging presence of great numbers of black women in the workforce beginning with World War II had some effect on the overall state of black mental health? How did the rise of feminism dur-

ing the 1970s effect relationships between black men and black women? And
how has the growth of the African-American middle class affected the mental health of blacks?

Assessing the current status of black men and black women—and the
points at which their educational, family, religious, and economic conditions coincide and diverge—is a necessary part of the search to unravel the
causes of black suicide. There is much about the interaction of gender, race,
and income and education levels, particularly as they influence blacks'
mental health and predisposition to self-destructive behavior, that has yet
to be understood.

However, the fact that black women are much less likely to kill themselves than black men is the one consistancy to be found among the many
variables of black suicide. In 1997, for example, the suicide rate among black
men aged twenty to twenty-four was 21.4 per 100,000, while for black
women in that age group the rate was 1.9, according to the U.S. Centers for
Disease Control. (And, interestingly, the suicide rate for black males and females aged twenty to twenty-four dropped during the mid-1990s: the suicide rate for black women between twenty and twenty-four declined from
2.9 in 1994 to 1.9 in 1997, while for black men in that age group the rate decreased from 24.7 in 1994 to 21.4 in 1997, still shockingly high.)[2] Several theories have emerged about the cause for this wide gap, but research has yet to
demonstrate, unequivocally, why black women are so much less inclined
toward suicide than black men. In general, women have lower rates of suicide than men, but the gap is wider among blacks. A look at overall suicide
rates in 1995 shows a rate of 19.7 per 100,000 for white men, compared to 4.4
for white women; the comparable black rates were 12.4 per 100,000 for black
men and 2.0 for black women.[3]

Following World War II, a theory to explain this gap emerged from a combination of sociological research and anecdotal reports that has since become conventional wisdom. It holds that black women—while experiencing
depression at a rate two times higher than that of black males (a proportion
that appears to be consistent across racial lines)—built networks of family,
religious, and social ties in the decades after slavery and Jim Crow that
served as emotional and psychological buffers to life-threatening behavior.
This theory also holds that black men—who have been physically and socially isolated through much of their history in America—have not developed similar buffers that might help them cope with the factors that pro-

duce stress-induced self-destructive behavior. In addition, some theorists have maintained that black males are more inclined to engage in types of suicidal behavior that are more violent, including life-threatening behaviors involving alcohol, drugs, and guns; studies show that black women attempt suicide more often than black men but are less likely to succeed in killing themselves.

Given the absence of solid statistical and long-term scientific analysis, it is entirely possible that this theory explains the disparity. At the same time, it is possible that the social-and-family-ties-as-protective factor scenario is too simplistic. We know that men, in general, are more violent than women, accounting for the bulk of violent crime in the United States, including homicide. Since suicide is a form of violence, it is not surprising that black male rates far exceed those of black females (just as the white male rates far exceed those of white females). And in our estimation, the underexplored reasons why African-American men might be more predisposed to engaging life-threatening behavior than black women are multifaceted and involve a range of biological and environmental factors—including hard-to-pin-down cultural and social-economic elements—that warrant a significant amount of additional research.

Berkeley psychologist Jewelle Taylor Gibbs asks, "Since both sexes are presumably exposed to the same 'protective' and 'risk factors,' (e.g., family structures, societal forces, and cultural values), what factors and concepts might account for the greater vulnerability of black males to commit suicide?" In a 1988 article in *Suicide and Life-Threatening Behavior,* the journal of the American Association of Suicidology, she added, "Although this is not a simple question to answer, some clues can be found in an analysis of several social indicators which suggest that young black males are at significantly higher risk than black females for a number of deviant and self-destructive behaviors."[4]

As we have discussed, many black Americans have internalized the belief that they are exceptionally strong, and over many decades have come to view themselves as being somehow inured to emotional stress. In the real world, African-Americans do exhibit an inner fortitude of the kind often found among people who are relegated to outsider status in a given society. This is a form of strength that is part of what W. E. B. DuBois defined as the "double consciousness" of blacks, a result of the experience of being an outsider in your own nation and of being required to manuever between and within two worlds. However, the responses of African-Americans to social pressure from racism and discrimination today are markedly different from those of their forbears. Developing and using the interpersonal and emotional skills that a black person needs to safely and productively make his or her way through life in postmodern America can be a difficult task.

For black males in particular, exercising impulse-control is vital for successful social interaction in the context of the larger society and requires true self-confidence, subtle language skills, and a degree of humility. While intelligence, physical strength, personal dignity, and religious faith undoubtedly helped many blacks to succeed in America in the past, the collection of social and psychological skills now required includes impulse control and socially directed critical thinking. Even following decades of advancement in nearly all sectors of American society, blacks are commonly confronted with white perceptions which stem from old stereotypes—that they are "angry" or that they have a "chip on their shoulder," for instance. Such perceptions can lead to awkward encounters in schools, the workplace, and in social settings. For African-Americans, the ability to ignore or overcome such perceptions on a regular basis could mean the difference between staying in school or dropping out, between keeping a job or being unemployed. And it is certainly true that the early influence of parents or family authority figures is of prime importance in the development of a child's social skills—especially their ability to cope with race-related issues. Is it possible, then, that the child-rearing practices of black parents produce different sets of coping skills for their male and female children? Do black boys and black girls receive different messages about how they should relate to other blacks? How they should relate to themselves? To white males and females, and to society as a whole?

Whatever the black child's gender, are the social skills and messages they receive adequate for the high-technology, hyperpolitical, hypersegregated environment of American classrooms, workplaces, and social spaces of the early twenty-first century? The question is complex and has only lately received the attention of the nation's sociologists and psychologists.

It is well known that in many communities black males carry the burden of being "cool," "hip," and "tough," which encourages them to develop social styles that may become self-destructive. These styles also fit poorly in the mainstream American cultural expectations for behavior in school and in the workplace.[5] For men in general, their sense of manhood requires that they be treated with dignity and respect, and for obvious historical reasons, black males are particularly sensitive to being "dissed" or emasculated by those who treat them as "boys." Many black males, particularly those from low-income backgrounds, counter images of weakness by adopting a bravado that may appear to be overly aggressive, especially to whites. In turn, whites and others may "protectively" avoid and discriminate against black men.

This too may be part of the picture, but before concrete links can be drawn between black male and female coping skills and the black suicide rate, as Taylor Gibbs has noted, the nation's mental health establishment must first devise a "multiple-factor, interdisciplinary theory to explain and predict suicidal behavior in black youth."[6]

The clinical mental health community was slow in charting the effects of post–civil rights era society on black mental health even as circumstances continued to alter the cultural and environmental landscape for black men and women in America. After the 1960s, the lessening influence of traditional social supports that many suicidologists believe helped keep the black suicide rate relatively low for so long—protective factors provided by closeness within the segregated black community and by the church—coincided with an increase in women and middle-class blacks entering colleges and corporate America. Between the late 1970s and late 1990s, the black homicide rate escalated, as did the suicide rate, mortality increases which coincided with a rise in the number of black female-headed households, a decline in the quality of inner-city schools, and an explosion of the illegal drug trade and black male incarceration rates.

These trends appear to be tied to economic causes but, once again, without long-term interdisciplinary surveys that correlate to black psychology, drawing absolute conclusions about their possible influence on male-female black suicide rates are highly problematic and politically risky. However unpleasant it is to consider, there exists a harsh reality known as the "crabs in the bucket" syndrome, wherein members of lower-caste groups not only fight desperately over the few dregs available to them, but also demonstrate cunning betrayal of their brethren in order to "climb out of the bucket" to a higher status. Encouraging such conflict has also been a "divide and conquer" strategy used by oppressors in many times and places. Theorists and clinical professionals, then, must be particularly sensitive to avoid the perception that they are pitting one gender against another in the quest to diagnose or treat mental health conditions. For example, would it be beneficial in the long term to remind a depressed, unemployed black male patient of the possibility that he is less appealing to white employers than black women because white employers are more likely to regard him as a physical threat? Or would the wiser strategy involve a focused attempt to help the depressed, unemployed black male patient build the kinds of skills he'll need to secure a job in the white-dominated workforce?

Indeed, a 1978 book by a black woman who sought to describe socioeconomic and sexual "tension" between post–civil rights era black men and women caused a heated controversy among both blacks and whites. In *Black Macho and the Myth of the Super-Woman,* Brooklyn writer Michele Wallace stirred up a hornet's nest of psychosocial and sexual angst surrounding black male and black female relationships. Interestingly, Wallace used the language of self-annihilation to communicate her premise:

> I am saying . . . that for perhaps the last fifty years, there has been a growing distrust, even hatred, between black men and black women. It has been nursed along not only by racism on the part of whites but also by an almost deliberate ignorance on the part of blacks about the sexual politics of their experience in this country. As the Civil Rights Movement progressed, little attention was devoted to an examination of the historical black male/female relationship, except for those aspects of it that reinforced the notion of the black man as the sexual victim of "matriarchal" tyranny. The result has been calamitous. The black woman has become a social and intellectual suicide; the black man, unintrospective and oppressive.[7]

Wallace's painful memoir examining black gender relationships contributed to an intra-racial flap that amounted to a twenty-year cold war between black male and female intellectuals and to a veritable moritorium on any meaningful research geared toward assessing the historic, biological, economic, and cultural influences affecting the state of black male and female mental health in general, and its impact on suicide rates in particular. Any consideration of the extremely personal nature of Wallace's book was lost amid the political heat it generated. Moreover, *Black Macho* followed another seemingly damning black woman's take on black male/female relations–playwright Ntozake Shange's groundbreaking *for colored girls who have considered suicide / when the rainbow is enuf.*[8] As with Wallace's personal and observational book, Shange's verse play sparked wide interest in the complexities of black male/female relationships, and these and other works engendered much political posturing by black academics and by white feminists who seemed to take the two works as solid proof that black men, like white men, had conspired for centuries to hold women down. Unfortunately, while open discussion of gender-related psychosocial issues is a good idea, the dearth of sound scholarly research on these matters produced a gap in understanding that continues to influence the current public perception of mental health and self-destructive behaviors in black men and women.

Therefore, our assessment of the cultural, socioeconomic, and ecological impacts on black mental health and their relationship to suicidal behavior must be drawn from other primary sources, including racially specific psychological studies and suicide research, evidence regarding gender-related economic and educational trends, and individual case studies drawn from personal experience and from the media. In total, a picture emerges in which historic disparities between black male and female suicide rates do seem to run parallel with economic and social trends. For example, consider that numerous census data show that black women attained higher education and entered the white-collar workforce in greater numbers than black men during the 1980s and 1990s. Black men, it seemed, were falling behind white men, white women, and black women in terms of achieving advanced college degrees and integrating into the white- and "pink"-collar workforces. During that same twenty years, between 1980 and 2000, the suicide rate for black males in their twenties climbed dramatically, reaching nearly 25 per 100,000 individuals by the end of the 1990s, while for black females in their twenties the rate was relatively stable, usually falling below 5 suicides per 100,000 during the same period.[9]

At the same time, since these economic and demographic trends have not been accompanied by interlocking surveys of black mental health, it is difficult to draw conclusions or project the outcome for the future health of African-Americans overall. Nevertheless, there are strong indications that the nexus of social, economic, and educational factors has significant bearing on the disparity between black male and black female suicide rates. And in the aggregate, following more than three hundred years of harsh social and economic conditions, it should not be surprising to learn that African-

American men in particular are reluctant to seek mental health services, as they associate the expression of emotional or psychological (dis)stress with personal weakness.

Conversely, black women, in keeping with the behavior of the total female population, have demonstrated more willingness than their male counterparts to engage close friends and family members during times of severe psychological stress. More difficult to identify, are the differences between black men and black women in terms of their willingness or ability to "reach out" beyond friends and family when experiencing emotional distress. While black women have historically shown a high degree of reluctance to seek mental health assistance, according to some signs that have emerged during the past decade they have begun seeking out medical professionals to help them cope with psychological problems in growing numbers. Popular black magazines, such as *Essence* and *Ebony,* for instance often focus on psychological issues. Still, there is much about the psychodyamic differences between black male and black female responses to depression and emotional conflict that has yet to be explored. What are the "breaking points," for example, that might lead black men to seek help, versus the "breaking points" for black women?

Black psychotherapist Julia A. Boyd, in her 1998 book *Can I Get a Witness: For Sisters, When the Blues Is More Than a Song,* details her own struggle with depression and emotional isolation, as well as the similar experiences of many of her female African-American clients. Chief among the obstacles to effective clinical treatment that black women face, Boyd writes, is the familiar, deeply ingrained belief that to show emotional distress is to admit to personal weakness and moral fallibility. Boyd notes that a kind of fatalistic reverence for the hardships black women have endured contributes to a general reluctance to seek professional help for depression. And while she fails to tackle the question of why black women seem to be more willing than black men to overcome this historic self-perception and get help when the emotional chips are down, Boyd's observations are instructive:

> Each week in my clinical practice, I encounter a significant number of sisters who present various symptoms on a clinical continuum from vague feelings of unhappiness to serious forms of physical illness, all of which include some form of depression. When presented with the assessment of depression, it's not uncommon, as I myself experi-

enced, that there's often a period of denial during which we struggle
with our thoughts and feelings surrounding our beliefs about being
strong Black women, and having an illness that we've long associated
with weakness of the lowest kind. . . . As Black women, we want to believe that our historical lineage of survival coupled with our indomi-
table strength of spirit will protect us from what we consider to be a
personal weakness. . . . Our fears about craziness, laziness, of being a
failure or weak keep us from accepting what is true. Our fear of wearing yet another "label" attached to our ethnicity and gender as Black
women has locked many of us into a state of helpless and sometimes
hopeless confusion concerning our emotional well-being.[10]

In Boyd's Seattle-based clinical psychotherapy practice, she has also observed a strong link between low self-esteem and depression in her clients,
a connection that is born out by numerous psychological and psychiatric
studies of blacks and whites, men and women over the last hundred years.
Regarding the particulars of black male and black female suicide, it is
important to consider the possible connections between low self-esteem,
depression, and an individual's environmental circumstances–including
their family's mental health history and the individual's socioeconomic status. A dearth of black male–oriented medical and mental health studies (or
even books by black male authors), however, leaves significant gaps in our
understanding of why black males appear to be more resistant than black
females to the idea of seeking help from medical or mental health professionals.

In recent years, some research into the possibility that gender-specific
biological factors (including neurological and hormonal influences) may
have some bearing on an individual's mental health has added new variables to the general field of suicidology. This possibility requires much more
investigation. In the meantime, it is helpful to consider the possible influences of the psychosocial elements that likely contribute to the disparity in
suicide rates, namely the differing responses to cultural pressures exhibited by black men and black women. In that regard, we might examine the
cultural and social climate during the most recent period in which the suicide rates of black males in their twenties escalated: the twenty-year period
between the late 1970s and the late 1990s. How did the social conditions for
black men and black women change during this period?

Some hints may be found in the experiences of two young black athletes who killed themselves during the waning years of the 1990s. Their stories are tragic in the Shakesperean sense, in that both young adults rose from humble circumstances to reach the heights of socially acceptable achievement, in this case athletics, only to crash to the depths of despair and take their own lives while still young.

In January of 1999, twenty-three-year-old Katrina Price shot and killed herself following the news that the professional basketball team she played on had shut down. Katrina's suicide came several months after the deaths of her mother and father, and was a cause for sad introspection for her friends and college community at the small university in Nacogdoches, Texas, where she had been an All-American. In the days before her suicide, Katrina had experienced a sudden weight loss that drew the concern of her friends and teammates. Yet no one seemed to realize the extent of her inner turmoil, according to a January 23, 1999, article in the *New York Times*. When asked about the weight loss, the young woman gave a vague answer. "If this had been anyone other than Katrina, it may have worried me," said Kristen Armor Webb, a longtime friend. "In hindsight, maybe I should have asked more about the [demise of her professional ball club following the deaths of her parents] but Katrina was also a private person. In all the years I've known her, I can't say whether or not she had a boyfriend. . . . But believe me, no one would have thought she was capable of something like this."

Without firsthand knowledge of Katrina's state of mind, we cannot know the exact causes of her fatal decision. Yet the accumulation of several elements that are known to contribute to depression and suicide–loss of loved ones, the end of an important relationship–almost certainly triggered other psychological stress within Katrina. And of particular importance, in our estimation, is the fact that Katrina chose a method of suicide that was brutally final: a shotgun.

The 1998 suicide of Tennessee high school football star Tito Lee supports the idea that socioeconomic influences–particularly the stress that derives from working one's way out of a predominantly black, low-income environment into a middle- or upper-income level that is predominantly white–may combine with unknown biological or psychological influences to portend an increase in black youth suicides.

Unlike Katrina Price, who graduated near the top of her class from Aus-tin State University, the nineteen-year-old stand-out football player from West Nashville had a spotty academic record. He didn't adjust well to the rigors of the Georgia Military College in Milledgeville, the school he at-tended after starring in linebacker and fullback positions during his time in secondary school at the upper middle-class, predominantly white Brent-wood Academy. Because he needed to improve his grades, Tito had gone to Georgia Military as a stopgap between high school and a major college. But he fled Milledgeville shortly after arriving in 1997, telling his friends and family that he was going to move back home temporarily, get a job, and take classes at a junior college located forty miles outside of Nashville.

Then, in July of 1998, he gave both his championship football rings to one of his three brothers and told family members that he was ready to drive to Middle Tennessee State University and enroll fulltime. As his parents helped him pack his car for the trip, Tito told them he'd forgotten something and went to his bedroom. That afternoon, on August 3, 1998, his mother found him dead from a gunshot wound to his head. He had found the fam-ily's pistol and killed himself, leaving behind a note written for his parents; according to an August 17, 1998, account in *Sports Illustrated,* Tito wrote in the note that he loved them. Reflecting the responses of his friends and fam-ily members, *Sports Illustrated* titled its article on Tito Lee "Nobody Saw It Coming."

Two cases of suicide attempts, by a black man and a black woman in the late 1990s, provide further insight into the kinds of stressors that can lead indi-viduals to contemplate self-murder. The fact that both had achieved a high degree of professional recognition again raises questions about what socio-economic events might trigger psychological and/or biological problems within some individuals.

On November 14, 1999, a nineteen-year-old black basketball star named Leon Smith swallowed more than two hundred aspirin tablets. When emer-gency paramedics arrived at his Dallas apartment they found the lanky youth dabbed in war paint and rambling that he was an Indian fighting Christopher Columbus. Weeks earlier, Leon, who hailed from a broken family and had lived in foster homes for much of his young life, had signed a $1.4 million contract with a professional basketball team. He had decided to skip college and take the route of increasing numbers of athletically talented but academically challenged young black males who go directly from high school sports into professional sports.

Ultimately, the pressure of the transition from his unstable living situation to the life of a pro basketball player took an enormous toll on Leon. In numerous media accounts, friends and family members spoke of him as being overwhelmed by circumstances. "I think Leon is on overload," said Doris Bauer, who was Leon's Chicago-based foster parent at the time of his attempted suicide. "He has this beautiful apartment and he's never lived in his own place."[11] Leon's inability to cope with sudden change and success exemplifies another pattern among blacks who kill themselves or attempt to do so, one that occasionally catches the eye of the media.

The experiences of Broadway and recording star Jennifer Holliday were chronicled in a story in the June 1999 issue of *Essence* magazine, which explored in vivid detail the phenomenon of depression among black females. In 1990, at the age of thirty, Jennifer had tried to kill herself in a Chicago hotel room by taking a handful of sleeping pills. This attempt followed years of inner struggles and professional triumphs for the talented singer. As an ingenue, she had appeared in one of the most beloved musicals of the late twentieth century, *Dreamgirls,* and earned a Tony Award for her performance. Despite that and other successes, Jennifer was constantly depressed and experienced severe weight fluctuations. Eventually she entered psychotherapy and began an antidepressant medication schedule that helped her cope with her emotional problems.

After several false starts with psychiatrists and other clinical professionals, Holliday was diagnosed as manic-depressive and came to view her ongoing psychopharmacological treatment as a difficult but manageable aspect of her life. Her odyssey demonstrates the importance of overcoming harmful stereotypes and the stigma of mental illness. "I didn't know how to explain to people why I just felt so sad all the time," Holliday told *Essence.* "People tell you, 'What do you have to be depressed about? Just snap out of it.' So I tried to deal with it myself. I didn't want to be labeled a loony bird or a cuckoo or something like that."[12] In 1999 Jennifer Holliday reached out to help other blacks cope with depression and suicidal ideas by appearing in a health promotion video sponsored by the National Medical Association that has since been distributed widely.[13]

Her experience also illustrates the consequences of the chemical imbalance that occurs in patients suffering from manic-depressive and other severe depressive disorders; these can be treated with many new forms of effective antidepressant drugs. These medications are often effective even when an individual becomes depressed due to severe external psychosocial stressors.

Obviously the circumstances of the preceeding cases were unique to those individuals. At the same time, we must pay closer attention to the nexus between economic, social, and biological causes as they relate to the mental health status of black men and women. "The blues" knows no gender boundaries, as many black musicians have artfully explored. The question facing the mental health establishment is whether it can learn to appreciate the nuanced shadings of the feelings described as the blues—and the subtleties of many other manifestations of mental distress, including self-destructive behaviors, among African-Americans.

Depression can be successfully treated with new drugs and other methods of therapy. Because severe depression is painful, debilitating, and may lead to suicide, it is critical that African-Americans, males and females, young and old, overcome their resistence to seeking help.

8

The Road Ahead

Society's Role in Prevention and Treatment

At this point in history it should be clear to all that African-Americans have suffered formidable mental stresses that have been in part the manifestation of the legacies of slavery (posttraumatic slavery syndrome) and in part the outcome of the twin burdens of poverty and racism.

The impact of racism itself, independent of poverty, still appears to exact a toll on the minds and bodies of the descendants of men and women brought to this continent as slaves, straining their capacity to adapt successfully in America. Researchers believe that racism has contributed to the high rates of hypertension, heart disease, and other stress-related illnesses in the black community. Psychologists have argued that long after emancipation and the end of legal segregation, the conflicts inherent in being black in America have led many black people to attempt to escape from the pressure of being second-class citizens through the use of drugs, alcohol, and other forms of self-destructive behaviors, including suicide (and homicide). And, as we have explored, black skepticism toward the medical-scientific community and reluctance to seek health care—also in part the outcomes of racism and discrimination—have compounded these problems.

In addition to examining other self-destructive behaviors among African-Americans, a major focus of our discussion has been the rapid rise in the suicide rate among young black men during the past several decades, a period during which many racial barriers were toppled and opportunities for some segments of the black population improved considerably. As the size of the black middle class has more than doubled in the last thirty-five years,[1] it would seem that there should be many reasons for renewed hope and contentment among the black population. Unfortunately, even with these gains, blacks continue to lag significantly behind whites in income, wealth, and education.

In exploring the causes of the rise in black suicide, we have discovered that explanations for the increase are not simple: they are multilayered, complex, and not exclusively tied to income or education levels. However, we have learned that during times of rapid advancement and high expectations, some blacks may feel greater despair at being left behind at lower economic and education levels than they had hoped for, or experience frustration that they have not advanced sufficiently in their occupations because of real or perceived racism. And whatever their achievements, modest or grand, too many blacks may still harbor feelings of inferiority and fear of failure. The complex interactions of many variables—racial, economic, psychosocial, and political—make it difficult to make generalizations that would explain every black suicide. Nevertheless, we have gained some insight into the confluence of stresses, internal and external, that push some individuals over the precipice to seek death by their own hands.

In many of our discussions, we linked black suicide rates with the high rates of homicide and substance abuse among blacks, which we identify as major expressions of self-destructive behavior among African-Americans dating from the time of slavery. Risky lifestyles are often ultimately lethal and are to some degree connected to internalized feelings of self-hatred and hopelessness; feelings of low self-worth can cause some black people to devalue not only their own lives but the lives of others; violence can be an expression of rage turned inward or outward, culminating in suicide or homicide. Some have speculated that the fact that blacks most often kill other blacks reflects a twisted form of suicide.

The association between self-destructive violence and suicide is worth exploring. Consider that when blacks rioted "against the system," in dozens of major cities in the 1960s, and in Miami and Los Angeles during the 1980s and 1990s, the businesses and homes they burned down were in their own communities.[2] The catastrophic effects of their rage included the destruction of stores owned by whites and other outsiders but overwhelmingly left the rioters' own neighborhoods looking like war zones; in the long term, the damage they inflicted was mainly on themselves.

Understanding the connection between black anger and inflicting violence on oneself–and people like oneself–is critical if we are to understand black suicide and other self-destructive behaviors. In seeking a possible means to prevent such tragedies, we must at least attempt to grasp and acknowledge this connection.

Some psychologists view all suicide as rage turned on the self, while in homicidal violence rage is "acted out" externally, on others. In a study by Herbert Hendin in the late 1960s, many blacks who had committed suicide were found to have histories of either actual or fantasized violence toward others.[3] Other data from the general population show a significant number of murder/suicides, particularly in cases of domestic violence. That suicide and homicide, in the final analysis, are both acts of violence must be incorporated into community strategies for suicide as well as homicide prevention.

Although depression is often the major psychological symptom preceding suicide, it is evident that in many suicides, especially among blacks, free-floating rage turned inward emerges as the paramount dynamic. In particular, impulsive suicides committed in anger can be seen in this light; they are common among young men who may lack mature internal controls. Other precursors of suicidal intentions, such as profound feelings of helplessness, entrapment, and hopelessness, are also critical. There is no doubt that such emotions are present in many suicides, but they may be difficult to uncover because individuals often refuse to acknowledge or express feelings that they fear will show weakness, a tag that could lead to their stigmatization in the community.

In addition, historically blacks have spoken of depression in terms of "feeling the blues" or "feeling down"–language that may not immediately suggest that a person is in need of psychological help. And, traditionally blacks have used informal networks–family, relatives, friends, and ministers–to obtain help for personal and family problems. Many still feel that seeking psychiatric help stigmatizes them as being "crazy." Fortunately, we have seen signs lately that some blacks, particularly those with higher levels of education, are more comfortable in seeking professional counseling than African-Americans have been in the past. For example, *Essence* and

Ebony, both popular-audience magazines, carry psychological advice columns and regularly refer readers to seek psychotherapy. And over the years, coauthor Alvin Poussaint has seen an increase in blacks seeking therapy either from him or by referral; he notes that reports from his clinical colleagues indicate that their caseloads of black patients have also grown. Moreover, a significant increase in the number of black therapists during the second half of the twentieth century has helped make this form of treatment more accessible and attractive to African-Americans.

Besides the fear of embarrassment in seeking help from mental health practitioners, we have reviewed other reasons why many blacks harbor a fear and distrust of health institutions in general. The history of a segregated health care system in the South, which ended little more than thirty years ago, causes blacks to wonder if their lives are valued and whether they will receive proper treatment while in the hands of medical professionals. African-Americans are aware that they have been used as guinea pigs in documented unethical medical research experiments. And even today studies show that in some of our best hospitals black patients do not always receive the same advanced diagnostic evaluations and medical treatments as white patients do.

Inevitably, such confirmations of current neglect of black clients will continue to deter some black people from seeking the help they need from institutions they mistrust. Further, health care practitioners and institutions must be aware of the day-to-day put-offs that continue to discourage blacks from partaking of their services.

For example, some African-American clients report negative experiences with white therapists, saying they have felt rejected, unwelcomed, or patronized. There is also evidence that blacks are sometimes misdiagnosed and put in more severe psychiatric diagnostic categories than whites who exhibit similar symptomatology. For instance, it has been generally found that clients with psychotic symptoms such as delusions and hallucinations are more likely to be perceived as schizophrenic if they are black, while whites are more likely to be seen as manic or severely depressed. Throughout our history, black patients treated in mental health facilities have been twice as likely as whites to be initially diagnosed with schizophrenia. Using more objective testing, or more thorough evaluation, many of these "schizophrenics" were found to be suffering from other diagnoses—notably depression.[4]

Depression is a broad category and is generally regarded as an episodic rather than a chronic illness; and depression generally offers a better prognosis than schizophrenia. Unfortunately, blacks tend to seek treatment much later in the course of their illnesses, and therefore develop more severe symptoms. Nonetheless, there is still a consistent pattern of misdiagnosis of depression among African-Americans. And in part this dilemma reflects problems in mental health training, which until relatively recently depicted depression as an upper-class disease. Coauthor Alvin Poussaint observed that as late as the 1960s psychiatrists in training were taught that clinical depression must be low among blacks because their suicide rate was only one-half that of whites. Some thought the incidence of depression was low because of special protective features of black family life and culture. Paradoxically, in other ways black culture has been seen by social scientists as a liability and risk factor for many social and mental dysfunctions.[5]

Overall, blacks have been evaluated from the perspective of a deficit model. During the 1960s, the phrase "culturally deprived" became a code term for poor minorities who were seen as lacking in intelligence and achievement because they failed to adopt the values and styles of the majority society. Implicit in the concept of "cultural deprivation" has been the assumption that the standards of the dominant white middle-class culture represent the norms by which all other classes and cultures may properly be measured. Therefore inner-city blacks were seen as culturally deprived rather than, more appropriately, as culturally different.

This disparaging perspective, which implied that blacks were deficient, no doubt reinforced the tendency of blacks to strive to be defensively "strong" and to deny emotional problems, particularly severe depression or psychotic symptoms. In the view of many blacks, admitting serious depression meant that one was unable to cope with life, and admitting such "weaknesses" gave rise to the possibility that one was indeed an inferior human specimen, just as the racists suggested. Black folklore and music, from spirituals to the blues to rap and hip-hop, conveyed to blacks that even under the worst of circumstances they must endure and overcome.

Institutional and societal stereotypes such as the image of the super-strong or the happy-go-lucky black are serious obstacles to promoting black mental health and require modification if we hope to stem the rising tide of suicide and other self-destructive behaviors among black youth. Mental health practitioners who are not part of the black experience need to become culturally competent professionals who avoid stereotypes. They must also appreciate the historical origins of the negative images blacks may have about their interactions with medical and mental health personnel. (And they should avoid taking such reluctance and trepidations personally; this in turn can result in negative feelings toward a patient). Therapists must be always cognizant that mental disorders occur in cultural contexts that may be very different from their own.

Because of negative past experiences with the health care system, blacks are inclined, in general, to be more fearful of psychologists and psychiatrists than white patients. In the past, particularly in the South, psychiatry was used as a weapon of social and political persecution of black citizens. As we've discussed, some white psychological theorists, under the guise of science, perpetuated myths of blacks' genetic inferiority and moral decadence. Even today, books like *The Bell Curve* (1994) have argued, with no valid scientific evidence, that black people are born, on average, intellectually inferior to whites.[6] With such negative images lingering and even predominating in the mainstream, mental health workers and law enforcement personnel are often inhospitable to blacks with mental health problems.

Blacks believe, rightly or wrongly, that they are not welcome in many community clinics and hospitals, and report an atmosphere of indifference or rudeness from white personnel.[7] It is apparent from anecdotal evidence that some African-Americans find white staff members to be either patronizing or overly fearful of blacks, particularly if a black client expresses anger or suspicion about clinic rules or services. They know that under certain circumstances white personnel may view them as dangerous and paranoid—and be influenced negatively when diagnosing the client. Some black outpatients have reported to coauthor Alvin Poussaint that they feared facing involuntary commitment to mental institutions because a mental health worker might describe them as a "danger to society."

In other instances, clinicians are reported to prescribe major antipsychotic tranquilizers instead of antidepressants for black patients who are agitated but suffering from severe depression rather than a thought disorder like schizophrenia. In addition, even before the era of managed care, blacks were more likely to be sent for treatment to drug clinics for pharmacological management rather than to centers where they could receive in-

tensive psychotherapy, which was considered by many clinicians to be the
better treatment. Because blacks came from cultural backgrounds with
different perspectives and styles than their white and/or middle-class clinicians, they were often dubbed "hostile," "not psychologically-minded,"
"not motivated for treatment," or too "passively uncooperative" to be suitable for psychotherapy.[8] Such practices openly and subtly deterred blacks
from seeking help because of the lack of comfort they felt in clinical
settings.

In addition to examining the negative experiences of African-Americans
in health facilities, we also identified the important task of reducing the
stigma and shame many blacks experience when they or a family member
have a mental problem. It is interesting that many blacks accept the notion
of a "nervous breakdown" (which they often see at least partly as a physical
condition), though they may hide such information and speak in whispers
about it, even among family members. Yet opportunities exist, particularly
with black news organizations, for the health care community and the nation's political leaders to present mental illnesses as diseases akin to physical medical conditions—as health concerns that are not signs of personal
weakness for which a person should feel ashamed.

Indeed, while there are environmental stresses that can precipitate a
mental illness, it must be communicated to the black community that many
mental dysfunctions represent imbalances in brain chemistry, including
illnesses such as depression and schizophrenia. Mental illnesses, in fact,
can be compared to the physiological imbalances that cause diabetes and
hypertension. People who come to appreciate mental conditions as primarily a manifestation of disrupted brain function will not feel that they are
emotionally troubled because of personal or moral deficiencies. With this
knowledge, they will be less likely to conclude that their suffering is due to
individual shortcomings or moral lapses that are entirely of their own
making.

Such educational efforts can help penetrate the wall of silence and
shame that blacks construct around mental disorders. These efforts should
include activism by all professionals but would be best accomplished under
the leadership of black psychiatrists, psychologists, social workers, and
ministers speaking out and writing about the care and prevention of mental
illness as health problems to which even the best of us can succumb. Mental
health professionals should also speak to community groups at local clubs,

schools, and churches, encouraging blacks to raise questions and concerns about mental illness in order to dispel the myths and ignorance that surround it.

Wherever possible, black professionals should make opportunities to appear on local TV and radio shows to talk about mental health issues among black Americans. National organizations such as the American Association of Black Psychologists, the Black Psychiatrists of America, the National Black Social Workers Association, and the National Medical Association (which in 1999 sponsored a video on depression among blacks)[9] should make print and video materials about mental health issues—including alcohol and drug abuse—available in the black community. Also, the general educational efforts made by the American Psychiatric Association and their counterparts in psychology and social work would be welcome support. Additionally, media and public service announcements by government health agencies would be of great benefit. With the Internet coming into greater use, mental health organizations can use interactive websites that allow individuals to obtain information about mental disorders and resources for help in the privacy of their homes. Although current studies have shown that fewer blacks have access to computers than whites, this will change in the years to come.[10] If vigorously undertaken, these initiatives will help to reduce the fear and stigma that envelop mental disorders for African-Americans—and may help deter suicide among blacks.

There are other concrete measures that might be taken. One way to increase the use of mental health services by black people may be to eliminate the term "mental health" from the titles of health clinics and hospital departments. Because of the stigma attached to that term, many blacks and others do not want to be seen going into such a facility. Some clinics have already changed their names to "Family Life Center" or "Family Learning Center," enabling clients to feel more comfortable walking in to talk about family and personal problems. Also, because of blacks' traditional involvement in churches, clinics in black communities should have guidelines that incorporate the spiritual element of their clients' lives as part of their diagnostic and treatment plans. Many patients get a great deal of psychological support from religion, while others may need to understand that their troubles are not due to sin or a punishment from God. Therapists, of course, should always show respect for the individuality and dignity of each of their patients and listen carefully to their perspectives on their own problems in order to construct an appropriate therapeutic plan that may involve the use of community resources and organizations, including the church.

Another important point to consider is that many black patients are put off by the indirect, distant style of traditional psychotherapy wherein the therapist rarely speaks while the patient does most of the talking and receives little feedback. More interactive approaches, including cognitive and behavioral therapies, may be more useful. Despite past negative experiences, blacks are likely to respond to a therapist's strong personal interest in them. This interest can be demonstrated, for example, by treating patients with courtesy and respect and even by engaging in friendly chit-chat at the beginning or end of each session.

Less formality, by which we do not mean patronizing over-familiarity, can be critical to many blacks' receptiveness to treatment, but most blacks, for historical reasons, would find it offensive for clinicians to address them by their first name instead of the more formal "Mr.," "Mrs.," or "Ms." And of course most adult blacks, even if quite young, would be angry if called "boy" or "girl" by white personnel. In decades of psychiatric work, coauthor Alvin Poussaint has encountered quite a number of cases where blacks did not return to clinics or psychotherapists when they were treated in what was or what was perceived to be a disrespectful manner.

Moreover, black people are more likely to believe that the health care establishment has a personal, caring interest in them when clinics are located in their community and staffed, at least in part, by people who look like them. The presence of minorities on staff can help to markedly improve black people's feelings of trust. They may also feel "safer" when they see minorities in positions of power and authority. Following the opening of community-based clinics several decades ago, more blacks have used these facilities for mental health services. Some clinics increase their appeal when they serve as family resource centers where case managers are on site to assist and collaborate with social services, welfare, hospitals, and other agencies with which their patients are involved. Such a full-service approach leads to more comprehensive care that takes into account the interrelatedness of the many environmental, social, and health problems affecting an individual's emotional well-being.

Making mental health facilities more accessible to black patients and other minorities is not just a question of geographic location but also a question of the makeup, style, and approaches of clinic personnel. To be sure, attempting to eliminate the cultural biases inherent in a white, Eurocentric-derived psychological and psychiatric tradition is a daunting task. But it is an effort that must be steadfastly pursued if all races and ethnicities are to be served effectively by today's mental health practitioners.

Many psychiatrists and psychologists acknowledge that, given the origin of their profession, traditional psychological principles are likely to be culturally biased. In the United States, mental health approaches are most often attuned to the white middle and upper classes and to those of higher educational background. Although the civil rights and black consciousness movements of the 1960s and 1970s stirred black psychiatrists and psychologists to make white therapists and others more aware of both overt and covert manifestations of racism, a great deal remains to be accomplished.[11]

All mental health practitioners are a product of their social conditioning and cultural mores, and many of them have been shaped in varying degrees by the white supremacist attitudes that have permeated American culture. Unfortunately, merely receiving psychiatric or psychological training does not purge a person of racist beliefs or stereotypes. As a consequence, blacks have suffered discrimination, sometimes intentional, sometimes unintended, from practitioners representing what most people feel should be the most people-sensitive branch of the health care system. As we have noted, many conflicts between black people and our mental health system have their roots in the past.

Throughout its history as a discipline, psychiatry has served as a mirror of social prejudices and cultural and political values. In twentieth-century America, psychiatrists, as sometimes unwitting supporters of the status quo, have created problems for the black community in its relationship to mental health concepts. The uneven training of many psychiatric workers has made it difficult for them to distinguish deviant, unhealthy behavior from what is merely culturally different behavior. For example, a young black man who believes that a white police officer might shoot him for the slightest indiscretion may not be paranoid, but such a feeling could be a sign of mental imbalance in a middle-aged white businessman. For many mental health practitioners it has taken a long time to realize that the life experiences of blacks differ from those of whites and that, as a result, so do their social and psychological adaptations and reactions.

Theorists and clinicians in psychology have been slow to update their practices to adequately assess and serve different cultural and socioeconomic groups. But today some training programs are beginning to offer more exposure to minority issues. Fortunately, recent forms of therapy such as cognitive, behavioral, and psychopharmacological treatments have made mental health care more available and suitable to wider populations. In the past few decades, it is fair to say, psychiatric institutions have made some gains in meeting the mental health needs of blacks and other minorities.

Nonetheless, there are still some mental health workers inclined to help blacks "adjust to their situation" while remaining unconcerned with eliminating racism in society or even in their own practices. We believe that there is a critical need for mental health professionals to serve as advocates for their clients whenever biased practices are discovered. There are a number of innovative measures that might be employed, but first the will must exist to update outmoded testing and diagnostic models.

Much psychological testing is based on standardization—the comparison of a person's responses to a standard, which may or may not have been developed with blacks and other minorities in mind. For example, the Minnesota Multiphasic Personality Inventory (MMPI), a widely used measure of personality functioning, originally (in 1943) had a femininity/masculinity scale that often depicted black men as feminine (defined as easily emotionally upset) because of sexist and cultural biases in the coded questions. This and similar problems with the MMPI have persisted in later versions of the test. "The MMPI asks a respondent to indicate whether statements apply to him. Rated as a 'feminine' sign is the choice of such statements as 'I would like to be a singer' and 'I think I feel more intensely than most people do,'" Alexander Thomas and Samuel Sillen pointed out in 1972. "Another test, the California Personality Inventory, gives a low-femininity rating to girls who do not fear thunderstorms or do not wish to be librarians."[12] Standardized intelligence (IQ) tests also abound with biases built into the testing and scoring that discriminate against blacks and other minority groups, who score lower than whites on average. Some efforts have been made during the past decades to standardize tests to a broader population base, but problems persist. Racist theorists continue to improperly use the IQ differences shown by such tests to postulate the genetic inferiority of blacks—even after researchers have acknowledged that there is no such thing as a "culture-free" test. This "scientific racism," restating in new terms that whites are superior, has been used by policymakers and private citizens to accept, without guilt, the continued oppression of and discrimination against blacks.[13]

However, the arrival of black clinical mental health specialists, while they are still a relatively small group, has had some positive effect. Until World War II there were few black psychiatrists to refute "scientific" racists, and they often worked in isolated predominantly white settings without significant contact with black colleagues. Since that time, however, the numbers of black psychiatrists and psychologists have steadily grown, albeit slowly. Today there are about 865 black psychiatrists (2.3 percent of the total number)[14] and about 1,375 black psychologists (1.6 percent of the total number)[15] practicing in America.

Over the past few decades many black psychiatrists and psychologists have joined the faculties of major universities and assumed administrative and policy-making roles. This has led to the increase in available black clinicians and an increase in research on minority mental health. Black mental health care providers have made their presence felt by publishing articles and books about the plight of blacks and the effects of white oppression. Articles have also appeared in the lay press and popular magazines. Some of these writings have influenced white and other minority therapists and the lay population. As a result, white attitudes within the mental health field are slowly changing for the better.

Moreover, in the spirit of multiculturalism, a group of Afrocentric theorists have proposed an African-derived psychology, separate from European-based psychology. Prominent among the cultural values advocated by these black psychologists are group-centered behavior, strong kinship bonds, a valuing of cooperation over competition, a "feeling" or affective orientation, and an overarching religious orientation that provides structure, direction, and a philosophy of the interrelatedness of all things.[16]

In their view, adherents of this school of psychology build on the strengths that have enabled African-Americans to cope effectively with the horrific and often brutal racism experienced during and after slavery. Afrocentric theorists argue that black psychology derives from the positive features of basic African philosophy, which dictate the values, customs, attitudes, and behavior of Africans in Africa and the New World. Many black clinicians are working toward the incorporation of some of these new perspectives into American psychiatry. While some Afrocentric therapists have totally rejected traditional Western psychiatry, perceiving it as yet another form of cultural genocide against African-Americans, the concept of a unique black psychology has been questioned by leading African and African-American psychiatrists who insist that although there are cultural differences in the clinical manifestations of emotional disorders, the underlying psychological mechanisms are similar across cultural lines. We are aligned with the latter group. Just as a purely European psychology is too narrow a model for all humanity, a purely African-based psychology is also too narrow for African-Americans because, as Americans, we have merged, whether by choice or force, with many cultures from around the world.

Although traditional psychiatry has not been responsive to the needs of blacks in America and many African-Americans have continued to turn to the church and the black minister, or even faith healers, palm readers, astrologers, and psychics, in recent years black Americans' interest in psychiatry has grown. Both middle-class and poor blacks have increased their utilization of psychological services.

A major challenge for the future will be in helping mental health providers develop the necessary skills to maintain therapeutic alliances with clients from different backgrounds. We urge practitioners to recognize and appropriately respond to verbal and nonverbal communications with their minority clients. Other important skills recommended by the Academy of Family Physicians and which we also endorse include:

- constructing a medical and psychosocial history and performing a physical examination in a culturally sensitive fashion
- using the bio-psychosocial model in disease prevention and health promotion, the interpretation of clinical signs and symptoms, and illness-related problem solving
- prescribing treatment in a culturally sensitive manner
- using the negotiated approach to clinical care
- using family members, community gatekeepers, language translators and interpreters, and other community resources and advocacy groups
- working collaboratively with other health care professionals in a culturally sensitive and competent manner
- working with alternative and complementary medical practitioners

and/or indigenous, lay, or folk healers when professionally, ethically, and legally appropriate

• identifying how one's cultural values, assumptions, and beliefs affect patient care and clinical decision making[17]

Ultimately, minority mental health practitioners have a special responsibility to encourage the adoption of these guidelines in professional organizations, training programs, hospital clinics, and managed care organizations. Clinicians with new insights will be better able to perceive self-destructive behaviors in blacks that are akin to suicide, as well as other clear indications of suicidal tendencies, for, as we have established, self-destructive acts can take many forms. Undoubtedly, some fatal accidents are suicides, and the self-damaging behavior of the alcoholic and the drug user can be considered a slow method of self-annihilation of the mind and body. Particularly with cocaine or heroin, it is almost impossible to determine whether death from an overdose was accidental or a suicide.

Individuals and the institutional community of health care practitioners must work together when faced with an individual in mental distress. To this end, local hospitals, church groups, and other civic agencies should supplement the work of clinics and prevention centers and provide information about services available to help the mentally troubled and those who feel the impulse to take their own lives. Psychiatric clinics have been inaccessible to young blacks for far too long, because of institutional and de facto racism, so community groups must advocate for clinic accessibility for their black constituents.

In doing so, community groups must campaign for adequate health care for all citizens. Thirty-one percent of minority adults aged eighteen to sixty-four do not have insurance, compared with 14 percent of white adults in the same age group.[18] The subject of universal health care is controversial and politically unpopular, yet we believe that any program that promotes universal health care will greatly benefit poor and minority communities. In addition, citizen groups should fight for parity in the coverage of mental illness in current health insurance plans. Currently many plans shortchange the mentally ill in comparison to the payments allowed for physical medical illness.

Blacks who feel trapped by undue social or legal hardships can be helped a great deal by agencies that provide legal aid, financial support, and guidance on coping with often indifferent government and business bureaucracies. The feeling that "there's no place to turn" can contribute to a sense of fatalism; for extremely troubled individuals bureaucratic unresponsiveness may even represent "the last straw."

Above all, we believe that the increase in suicide among young black males should be a wake-up call to the black community and to public health officials. And, as we have discussed, there is plenty of evidence to show that in fact the suicide rate among blacks is much higher than statistics indicate because of a historic underreporting of suicide among the African-American population.

Our tasks, then, in attempting to help stem the tide of black suicidal and other self-destructive behaviors (including homicide) should include the following:

1. Make mental health clinics and practitioners more accessible and user-friendly to black clients. Black people should be made aware, through educational programs and media outlets, that clinical depression can be treated with antidepressants and talk therapy. Treatment programs for alcoholism and drug abuse must also be available and accessible.

2. Remove the stigma from mental illness while simultaneously educating the black community to seek professional help in times of emotional crisis, particularly if they are depressed or irritable and have suicidal or homicidal thoughts.

3. Provide education and training to mental health practitioners to eliminate racist stereotyping and simultaneously promote the skills for delivering culturally competent care.

4. Use a public health approach to reduce the risk factors that heighten the likelihood of suicide, such as depression, psychotic disorders, alcoholism, drug abuse, and the easy availability of firearms.

5. Support educational programs in conflict resolution, anger management, and violence prevention.

6. Campaign for health insurance coverage for all citizens and demand parity in coverage for the treatment of mental illness under all insurance plans.

7. Continue, as a nation, to fight on all fronts—social, political, and economic—the racism and poverty that continue to damage blacks and others psychologically, and which perpetuate severe mental stresses in black communities already suffering from poor education and high rates of crime and violence.

Until the general quality of life improves for all in America, the best protections and deterrents to suicide and other self-destructive behaviors among black people include the development of strong kinship bonds within the family and community that foster a sense of group togetherness and caring attitudes. Groups focused on self-help and mutual aid are important for community mental health support programs.

Further, community-based organizations must join the government effort announced by President Clinton in February of 1998 to eliminate the health disparities experienced by racial and ethnic minority groups by the year 2010. All citizens must join together to support these efforts.

Indeed, as the health status of all Americans improves, we can anticipate in this new century a decline in the heart-wrenching self-destructive behaviors that have been so damaging to African-Americans. Then perhaps, as the Reverend Jesse Jackson Sr. so eloquently put it more than twenty years ago, it will be possible for even the most disenfranchised Americans to "keep hope alive."

9

Casting Off the Burden

Where to Find Help

O n July 28, 1999, United States Surgeon General David Satcher, along with Tipper Gore, wife of Vice President Al Gore, announced a national plan to prevent suicide in America. Speaking at a White House press conference, Dr. Satcher said, "For every two people who die by homicide in this country each year, three people commit suicide. We must continue to develop a national suicide prevention strategy but we must also do a better job right now of taking steps that we know can work."[1]

While the initiative announced by Dr. Satcher and Mrs. Gore marked a watershed in government leadership on national mental health issues, the plan did not offer strategies aimed specifically at addressing mental health concerns in minority communities. Nonetheless, the surgeon general announced a funding plan–$7.3 million for research at the National Institutes of Mental Health for prevention and treatment programs, and $17 million for suicide prevention research projects–to support programs in mental health care on the state and regional levels. We urge those working to implement the government's initiatives to pay particular attention to community-based programs that tackle the unique aspects of minority mental health problems. As we have outlined in this book, several unique features–including the history of slavery and segregation, and continuing racism and discrimination in America–combine with other risk factors such as depression, anger, drug and alcohol abuse, and easy access to fire-arms to make suicide and self-destructive behavior particularly complex issues within the black community. Additionally, as the surgeon general has rightly pointed out, the stigma surrounding mental illness is particu-larly damaging to efforts to prevent suicide; this stigma, while not unique to blacks, is especially powerful among African-Americans.

In total, the government's new emphasis on improving mental health care across the United States is encouraging. The added funding and re-newed effort by public health officials should increase public awareness about the obstacles that prevent many Americans from receiving the men-tal health care they need. In minority communities especially, questions surrounding access, affordability, and the absence of culturally competent psychological care are particularly troubling. In many communities, the people working on the few initiatives that are in place to serve the treatment needs of blacks and other underserved groups face the tough tasks of over-coming limited funding as well as struggling to reduce the stigma that de-ters clients from seeking help.

In Boston, for example, the Roxbury Community Health Center (located in a predominantly black community) provides mental health services, in-cluding youth counseling, suicide prevention programs, and drug abuse counseling. The center is careful to exclude the term "mental health" from most of its public titles and public service literature lest patrons feel hesi-tant about entering a building clearly marked with those words. Neverthe-less, many residents rely on the Center for help with health, mental health, and social service needs.

Ultimately, government and local public and private health officials must establish permanent programs that focus on improving mental health services in underserved communities. Yet individuals experiencing mental distress should avail themselves of whatever services are now available. The alternative—suffering in silence—is counterproductive to their health.

If you are suicidal, call the national hotline:
1-800-SUICIDE (1-800-784-2433)

OTHER SOURCES OF HELP AND INFORMATION

1000 Deaths (website)
http://www.1000deaths.com/
This site is devoted to raising awareness of survivor issues and offering comfort and support to those who have lost a loved one to suicide. Good source of support and information for survivors. The title comes from the realization that a survivor dies a thousand deaths trying to understand why their loved one committed suicide.

About Elder Suicide: An Introduction to a Late-Life Tragedy
http://members.tripod.com/~LifeGard/elder.html
Informational website by Tony Salvatore on why "elder suicide" may be overlooked. It looks at the possible causes and also gives advice on what to look for in an elderly person in order to prevent suicide.

American Academy of Child and Adolescent Psychiatry
3615 Wisconsin Avenue N.W.
Washington, D.C. 20016-3007
202-966-7300

Facts for Families
1-800-333-7636
http://www.aacap.org/publications/factsfam
"The Depressed Child" and "Teen Suicide" are brochures designed to educate parents and families about psychiatric disorders affecting children and adolescents. The "Facts for Families" series covers a wide range of issues.

American Association of Suicidology
Office of the Executive Director
4201 Connecticut Avenue, N.W., Suite 408
Washington, D.C. 20008
202-237-2280
Fax: **202-237-2282**
http://www.suicidology.org/contact.htm
The American Association of Suicidology is dedicated to the understanding

and prevention of suicide. AAS promotes research, public awareness programs, education, and training for professionals and volunteers. In addition, it serves as a national clearinghouse for information on suicide.

American Foundation for Suicide Prevention
120 Wall Street, 22nd floor
New York, NY 10005
888-333-2377 or **212-363-3500**
Fax: 212-363-6237
http://www.afsp.org
The American Foundation for Suicide Prevention is dedicated to advancing our knowledge of suicide and our ability to prevent it. Provides state-by-state directories of survivor support groups for families and friends. Also provides information regarding suicide statistics, prevention, and surviving.

Anxiety Disorders Association of America
11900 Parklawn Drive, Suite 100
Rockville, MD 20852
www.adaa.org
ADAA promotes the prevention and cure of anxiety disorders and works to improve the lives of all people who suffer from them. The association is made up of professionals who conduct research and treat anxiety disorders and individuals who have a personal or general interest in learning more about such disorders.

Association of Black Psychologists
P.O. Box 55999
Washington, D.C. 20040-5999
202-722-0808
National organization of black psychologists focusing on minority mental health issues.

Black Psychiatrists of America
Altha Stewart, M.D., President
Detroit Wayne County CMH Agency

640 Temple, 8th Floor
Detroit, MI 48201
National organization of black psychiatrists focusing on minority mental
health issues.

    Centers for Disease Control and Prevention,
    National Center for Injury Prevention and Control
National Center for Injury Prevention and Control
Division of Violence Prevention
Centers for Disease Control and Prevention
Mailstop K60
4770 Buford Highway
Atlanta, GA 30341-3724
770-488-4362
www.cdc.gov/ncipc
Provides information on suicide and violence, violence prevention, and
related issues. Publications include "Suicide Among Black Youths: United
States, 1980–1995" (March 20, 1998) and "Suicide Among Black Youths" (fact
sheet) (March 20, 1998).

    Depression and Related Affective Disorders Association (DRADA)
Meyer 3-181, 600 North Wolfe Street
Baltimore, MD 21287-7381
410-955-4647 (Baltimore, MD)
202-955-5800 (Washington, D.C.)
www.med.jhu.edu/drada
Organization of people with depression or manic-depressive illness, family
members of persons with the illness, professionals working with the illness. Its mission is to alleviate the suffering arising from depression and
manic depression by assisting self-help groups, providing education and
information, and lending support to research programs.

    Gay Bisexual Male Youth Suicide Studies
http://www.virtualcity.com/youthsuicide/
Informational website regarding gay and bisexual male suicide problems
and related issues.

Have a Heart's Depression Resource
http://www.have-a-heart.com
Website described as a rest stop for the depressed and suicidal. This site presents various articles on depression and suicide/suicidal thoughts. It is also a guide to lead the depressed to helpful resources. All articles are written by the site's author, who has personal experience with these subjects.

Internet Mental Health
http://www.mentalhealth.com/fr20.html
This website has helpful information and a variety of links to additional information and support resources.

Mental Health Net
http://mentalhelp.net/guide/suicidal.htm
Website providing resources and information on suicide and depression. This is a good place to start to obtain information and support.

Metanoia
http://www.metanoia.org/suicide/
Website designed to help people who are considering suicide. Very supportive site.

National Alliance for the Mentally Ill
Colonial Place Three
2107 Wilson Boulevard, Suite 300
Arlington, VA 22201-3042
Toll-free helpline-**1-800-950-NAMI (6264)**
Office: **703-524-7600**
Fax: **703-524-9094**
http://www.nami.org/update/suicide.html
The National Alliance for the Mentally Ill (NAMI) is a nonprofit, grassroots, self-help support and advocacy organization of consumers, families, and friends of people with severe mental illnesses.

National Depressive and Manic-Depressive Association
730 N. Franklin Street, Suite 501
Chicago, IL 60610-3526

800-826-3632 or 312-642-0049
Fax: 312-642-7243
www.ndmda.org
National DMDA is a not-for-profit organization established to educate patients, families, and the public concerning the nature and management of
depressive and manic-depressive illness as treatable medical diseases, foster self-help for patients and families, eliminate discrimination and stigma
associated with these illnesses, improve access to care, and advocate for research toward the elimination of these illnesses.

National Institute on Alcohol Abuse and Alcoholism (NIAAA)
6000 Executive Boulevard–Willco Building
Bethesda, MD 20892-7003
www.niaaa.nih.gov
The NIAAA supports and conducts research on the causes, consequences,
treatment, and prevention of alcoholism and alcohol-related problems. NI-
AAA also provides leadership in the national effort to reduce the severe and
often fatal consequences of these problems.

National Institute on Drug Abuse
6001 Executive Boulevard
Bethesda, MD 20892-9561
301-443-1124
www.nida.nih.gov
NIDA's mission is to bring the power of science to bear on drug abuse and
addiction. This charge has two components. The first is the strategic support and conduct of research across a broad range of disciplines. The second is to ensure rapid and effective dissemination and use of research findings in order to improve drug abuse and addiction prevention, treatment,
and policy.

National Institute of Mental Health (NIMH)
Suicide Research Consortium
NIMH Public Inquiries
6001 Executive Boulevard, Room 8184, MSC 9663
Bethesda, MD 20892-9663
301-443-4513

Fax: 301-443-4279
www.nimh.nih.gov/research/suicide.htm
Provides information on specific mental disorders, including their diagnosis and treatment.

National Organization for People of Color Against Suicide, Inc.
(NOPCAS)
P.O. Box 125
San Marcos, TX 78667
830-625-3576
DB31@swt.edu
NOPCAS is a support and advocacy organization for family members and loved ones of individuals who have committed suicide. (It welcomes white survivors of suicide but is primarily geared toward minorities who have lost loved ones to suicide.) Along with offering support for family members of suicides, its goal is to raise awareness of depression, mental illness, and suicidal behavior in minority communities. It was founded in the early 1990s by Donna Holland Barnes, Ph.D., Doris Smith, and Les Franklin, all of whom lost sons to suicide. The group has members across the United States and holds an annual conference. It plans to raise money to fund research into suicide in minority communities.

National Suicide Prevention Directory (NSPD)
http://www.angelfire.com/biz/mereproject/nspdmain.html
The purpose of this website is to provide the public with a central source of contact information for suicide prevention organizations committed to providing educational and counseling programs aimed at long-term suicide prevention. The NSPD is designed to enable the public to have access to the information centers which are established to teach individuals how to recognize persons at risk and how to intervene in the lives of such persons before they make attempts to kill themselves. Site includes list of phone numbers to call for help in every state.

Samaritans of Boston
617-247-0220 (24-hour hotline)
Samariteen for teens: **1-800-252-TEEN**
500 Commonwealth Avenue

Boston, MA 02215
Business office: 617-536-2460
Suicide hotline.

SAVE Suicide Awareness Voices of Education
http://www.save.org/
The mission of the SAVE website is to educate the public about suicide prevention and to speak for suicide survivors. Offers helpful support for survivors.

Shaka Franklin Foundation for Youth
8101 East Dartmouth Avenue #11
Denver, CO 80231
303-337-2515
www.shaka.org
The Shaka Franklin Foundation for Youth was founded in 1995 after the suicide death of sixteen-year-old Shaka Franklin, by his father and community activist Les Franklin. The Foundation focuses on correcting the self-
destructive behavior of our young people (ages twelve to twenty-one) and
addressing the various problems in their lives that precipitate negative feelings which sometimes lead to suicide.

Substance Abuse and Mental Health Services Administration
(SAMHSA)
Room 12-105 Parklawn Building
5600 Fishers Lane
Rockville, MD 20857
301-443-8956
www.samhsa.gov
Provides information on substance abuse and mental health. Oversees the
Safe Schools/Health Students Initiative, a collaborative effort among the
Departments of Health and Human Services, Education, and Justice to provide grants to promote healthy childhood development and prevent violent
behavior. It also oversees the School Action Grant Program, a school violence prevention effort launched by the Centers for Mental Health Services
in collaboration with the Center for Substance Abuse Treatment to encourage communities to promote healthy childhood development and prevent
youth violence and substance abuse.

Suicide Prevention Advocacy Network (SPANUSA)
5034 Odin's Way
Marietta, GA 30068
Toll-free: 1-888-649-1366
Fax: 770-642-1419
www.spanusa.org
SPAN is a nonprofit organization dedicated to the creation of an effective national suicide prevention strategy. SPAN links the experience of those bereaved by suicide with the expertise of leaders in science, business, government, and public service to achieve the goal of significantly reducing the national rate of suicide by the year 2010.

U.S. Surgeon General
Dr. David Satcher
Office of the Assistant Secretary for Health/Surgeon General
202-690-7694
www.surgeongeneral.gov
Provides information on health and mental health. Information on the Surgeon General's initiative "National Strategy for Suicide Prevention" and "Call to Action to Prevent Suicide 1999" are available on the website (http://www.surgeongeneral.gov/library/calltoaction/default.htm).

RECOMMENDED READING

Our chapter notes list scholarly books and articles on suicide and mental health. The following books will provide helpful reading for individuals and families struggling with issues related to suicide in their own lives.

Black Man Emerging: Facing the Past and Seizing a Future in America, by Joseph L. White, James Henry Cones III, and James H. Cones (W. H. Freeman, 1999).

Boys into Men: Raising our African American Teenage Sons, by Nancy Boyd-Franklin, Ph.D., A. J. Franklin, Ph.D., with Pamela Toussaint (E. P. Dutton, 2000).

Brothers on the Mend: Understanding and Healing Anger for African-American Men and Women, by Ernest H. Johnson, Ph.D. (Pocket Books, 1998).

Can I Get a Witness?: For Sisters When the Blues Is More Than a Song, by Julia A. Boyd (E. P. Dutton, 1998).

Choosing to Live: How to Defeat Suicide through Cognitive Therapy, by Thomas E. Ellis, Psy.D. and Cory F. Newman, Ph.D. (New Harbinger Publications, 1996).

Death by Denial: Studies of Suicide in Gay and Lesbian Teenagers, edited by Gary Remafedi (Alyson, 1994).

Feeling Good Handbook, by David Burns (Plume, 1990).

Helping Your Child Cope With Depression and Suicidal Thoughts, by Tonia K. Shamoo et al. (Jossey-Bass, 1997).

Night Falls Fast: Understanding Suicide, by Kay Redfield Jamison (Knopf, 1999).

No One Saw My Pain: Why Teens Kill Themselves, by Andrew Slaby and Lili Frank Garfinkel (Norton, 1996).

No Time to Say Goodbye: Surviving the Suicide of a Loved One, by Carla Fine (Doubleday, 1999).

Out of the Nightmare: Recovery from Depression and Suicidal Pain, by David L. Conroy, Ph.D. (New Liberty Press, 1991).

Overcoming Depression, by Demitri and Janice Papolos (HarperCollins, 1997).

Speaking of Sadness: Depression, Disconnection, and the Meanings of Illness, by David Karp (Oxford University Press, 1996).

Suicide: The Forever Decision: For Those Thinking about Suicide, and for Those Who Know, Love, or Counsel Them, by Paul G. Quinnett (Crossroads, 1997).

What the Blues Is All About: Black Women Overcoming Stress and Depression, by Angela Mitchell and Kennise Herring (Perigee, 1998).

Willow Weep for Me: A Black Woman's Journey through Depression, by Meri Nana-Ama Danquah (Ballantine Books, 1999).

Notes

Introduction

1. United States Public Health Service, *The Surgeon General's Call to Action to Prevent Suicide* (Washington, D.C., 1999).

2. From the U.S. Centers for Disease Controls and Prevention, annual morbidity reports of 1998.

Chapter 1: "He Didn't Seem Depressed"

1. Douglas G. Jacobs, ed., *The Harvard Medical School Guide to Suicide Assessment and Intervention* (San Francisco: Jossey-Bass, 1999), 7.

2. Ibid., 6.

3. U.S. Public Health Service, *The Surgeon General's Call to Action to Prevent Suicide* (Washington, D.C., 1999).

4. On February 5, 1999, the National Organization for People of Color Against Suicide, Inc., held its second annual Survivors after Suicide Conference, at Clark/Atlanta University. During his address, Les Franklin discussed many aspects of black suicide, including recent rates of teen suicides and rates for Colorado teens. His source was the state of Colorado.

5. "State of Colorado Suicide Prevention and Intervention Plan," the report of the Governor's Suicide Prevention Advisory Commission, November 1998, p. 9 overleaf.

6. U.S. injury mortality statistics, from *Suicide 1997–1994,* National Cen-

ter for Injury Prevention Control, Centers for Disease Control at their website: http://www.cdc.gov/ncipc/data/us9794/Suic.htm.

CHAPTER 2: SUICIDE IN BLACK AND WHITE

1. U.S. Public Health Service, *The Surgeon General's Call to Action to Prevent Suicide* (Washington, D.C., 1999).

2. U.S. Centers for Disease Control and Prevention, Division of Violence Prevention, National Center for Injury Prevention and Control, *1998 Annual Suicide Report*.

3. Douglas G. Jacobs, ed., *The Harvard Medical School Guide to Suicide Assessment and Intervention* (San Francisco: Jossey-Bass, 1999), 41.

4. See U.S. Public Health Service, *The Surgeon General's Call to Action to Prevent Suicide* (Washington, D.C., 1999).

5. Douglas G. Jacobs, ed., *The Harvard Medical School Guide to Suicide Assessment and Intervention* (San Francisco: Jossey-Bass, 1999), 27.

6. Stephanie Strom, "In Japan, Mired in Recession, Suicides Soar," *New York Times*, 15 July 1999, 1.

7. Emile Durkheim, *Suicide: A Study in Sociology*, trans. John A. Spaulding and George Simpson (New York: Free Press, 1951).

8. David Lester, *Suicide in African-Americans* (Commack, N.Y.: Nova Science, 1998), 4.

9. David Lester, "Suicide in America: A Nation of Immigrants," *Suicide and Life-Threatening Behavior* 27, no. 1 (spring 1997): 52.

10. Sigmund Freud, "Mourning and Melancholia," in *Collected Papers*, vol. 4 (London: Hogarth, 1949).

11. Gregory Zilboorg, "The Sense of Immortality," *Psychoanalytic Quarterly* 7 (1938).

12. Alfred Adler, "Suicide," *Journal of Individual Psychology* 14 (1958): 57–61.

13. Sandor Rado, "Psychodynamics of Depression from the Etiologic Point of View," in *Psychoanalysis of Behavior*, vol. 1 (New York: Grune & Stratton, 1956).

14. E. S. Schneidman and N. L. Farberow, eds., *Clues to Suicide* (New York: McGraw-Hill, 1957).

15. M. Laufer and M. E. Laufer, *Adolescence and Developmental Breakdown* (New Haven, Conn.: Yale University Press, 1984).

16. John T. Maltsberger, "Pathological Narcissism and Self-regulatory Processes in Suicidal States," in *Disorders of Narcissism*, ed. E. F. Ronningstam (Washington, D.C.: American Psychiatric Press, 1998), 327–44.

17. Black/white suicide rates estimated by Lester in David Lester, *Suicide in African-Americans* (Commack, N.Y.: Nova Science, 1998), 60–70.

18. National Center for Health Statistics, *The National Vital Statistics Report* (Washington, D.C., 1999).

19. CDC, "Suicide among Black Youths–United States," *Morbidity and Mortality Weekly Report* 279, no. 18 (13 May 1998).

20. E. Stanley and T. Barters, "Adolescent Suicidal Behavior," *American Journal of Orthopsychiatry* 40 (1970): 87–96.

21. Orlando Patterson, *The Ordeal of Integration: Progress and Resentment in America's "Racial" Crisis* (Washington, D.C.: Civitas/Counterpoint, 1997), 29.

22. Paul C. Holinger, Daniel Offer, James T. Barter, and Carl C. Bell, *Suicide and Homicide Among Adolescents* (New York: Guilford Press, 1994).

23. Jack P. Gibbs, *Suicide* (New York: Harper & Row, 1969).

24. Pamela Belluck, "Black Youths' Rate of Suicide Rising Sharply," *New York Times*, 20 March 1998, 1.

25. Charles Prudhomme, "The Problem of Suicide in the American Negro," *Psychoanalytic Review* 25 (1938): 372–91.

26. M. H. Brenner, "Personal Stability and Economic Security," *Social Policy* 8, no. 1 (May/June 1977): 2–4.

27. *United States Bureau of Labor Statistics National Annual Report* (Washington, D.C., 1999).

28. H. F. Myers, "Stress, Ethnicity and Social Class: A Model for Research with Black Populations," in *Minority Mental Health*, ed. E. E. Jones and S. J. Korchin (New York: Praeger, 1982).

29. Arlene Levinson, "More Blacks, Hispanics, Go on to College, Study Finds," *Boston Globe*, 10 February 2000, "National Report."

30. Warren Breed, "The Negro and Fatalistic Suicide," *Pacific Sociological Review* 13 (1970): 156–62.

31. Lindsay M. Hayes, "National Study of Jail Suicides: Seven Years Later," *Psychiatric Quarterly* 60, no. 1 (spring 1989): 7.

32. Lindsay M. Hayes, "Prison Suicide: An Overview and a Guide to Prevention," by the National Center on Institutions and Alternatives, *The Prison Journal* 75, no. 4 (1995): 432.

33. Mark Mauer, *Intended and Unintended Consequences: State Racial Disparities in Imprisonment* (Washington, D.C.: The Sentencing Project, 1997), 3.

34. R. W. Maris, *Social Forces in Urban Suicide* (Homewood, Ill.: Dorsey, 1969).

35. Lindsay M. Hayes, "National Study of Jail Suicides: Seven Years Later," *Psychiatric Quarterly* 60, no. 1 (spring 1989): 19.

36. Carl C. Bell and Harshad Mehta, "The Misdiagnosis of Black Patients with Manic Depressive Illness," *Journal of the National Medical Association* 72, no. 2 (1980): 141–45. Carl C. Bell and Harshad Mehta, "Misdiagnosis of Black Patients with Manic Depressive Illness: Second in a Series," *Journal of the National Medical Association* 73, no. 2 (1981): 101–107.

37. Alvin F. Poussaint, "Black Suicide," in *Comprehensive Textbook of Black-Related Diseases,* ed. Richard Allen Williams (New York: McGraw-Hill, 1975), 707–14.

CHAPTER 3: "BOY, YOU MUST BE CRAZY"

1. Alexander Thomas and Samuel Sillen, "Challenge to the Profession," in *Racism and Psychiatry* (New York: Brunner/Mazel, 1972), 3.

2. William A. Hayes, "Radical Black Behaviorism," in *Black Psychology,* ed. Reginald L. Jones (New York: Harper & Row, 1972), 52.

3. Castellano B. Turner and Bernard M. Kramer, "Connections Between Racism and Mental Health," in *Mental Health, Racism and Sexism,* ed. Charles V. Willie, Patricia Perri Rieker, Bernard M. Kramer, Bertram S. Brown (University of Pittsburgh Press, 1995), 7.

4. Samuel Cartwright, "Report on the Diseases and Physical Peculiarities of the Negro Race," *New Orleans Medical and Surgical Journal,* May 1851, 707.

5. James Howard Jones, *Bad Blood: Tuskegee Syphilis Experiment* (Free Press, 1993).

6. Vanessa Northington Gamble, "Under the Shadow of Tuskegee: African Americans and Health Care," *American Journal of Public Health* 87, no. 11 (1997): 1775.

7. Ibid., 1774.

8. Castellano B. Turner and Bernard M. Kramer, "Connections Between

Racism and Mental Health," in *Mental Health, Racism and Sexism,* ed. Charles V. Willie, Patricia Perri Rieker, Bernard M. Kramer, Bertram S. Brown (University of Pittsburgh Press, 1995), 5.

9. Eugene Genovese, *Roll Jordan, Roll: The World the Slaves Made* (New York: Vintage Books, 1976).

10. Ibid.

11. Alexander Thomas and Samuel Sillen, *Racism and Psychiatry* (New York: Brunner/Mazel, 1972), 15.

12. From authors' phone interview with Dorothy Roberts, June 1999.

13. Kay Mills, *This Little Light of Mine: The Life of Fannie Lou Hamer* (New York: Plume, 1994).

14. Abram Kardiner and Lionel Ovesey, *The Mark of Oppression: Explorations in the Personality of the American Negro* (Cleveland: World Publishing Company, 1951), 297.

15. Kenneth B. Clark, *Prejudice and Your Child* (Middleton, Conn.: Wesleyan University Press, 1963).

16. William H. Grier and Price M. Cobbs, *Black Rage* (New York: Basic Books, 1968).

17. Charles Prudhomme, "The Problem of Suicide in the American Negro," *Psychoanalytic Review* 25 (1938): 372–91.

18. E. Franklin Frazier, *Black Bourgeoisie: The Rise of a New Middle Class in the United States* (Glencoe, Ill.: Free Press, 1957).

19. Kenneth B. Clark, *Dark Ghetto: Dilemmas of Social Power* (New York: Harper & Row, 1965).

20. Frantz Fanon, *The Wretched of the Earth* (New York: Grove Press, 1963).

21. Reginald L. Jones, *Black Psychology* (New York: Harper & Row, 1972).

22. Dorothy S. Ruiz, ed., *The Handbook of Mental Health and Mental Disorder among Black Americans* (New York: Greenwood, 1990).

23. A. T. Fort, J. C. Morrison, L. W. Diggs, S. A. Fish, and L. Berreras, "Counseling the Patient with Sickle Cell Disease about Reproduction: Pregnancy Outcome Does Not Justify the Maternal Risk," *American Journal of Obstetrics and Gynecology* 111, no. 3 (1971): 324–27.

24. Hilda F. Wiese et al., "Essential Fatty Acids in Infant Nutrition," *Journal of Nutrition* 66 (1958): 345–60.

25. Arild Hansen et al., "Role of Linoleic Acid in Infant Nutrition," *Pediatrics* 31, supplement 1, part 2 (1963): 170–92.

26. Kevin A. Schulman, Jessa A. Berlin, William Harless, et al., "The Effect of Race and Sex on Physicians' Recommendations for Cardiac Catherization," *New England Journal of Medicine* 340, no. 8 (1999): 621.

27. Ibid., 624.

28. Paul A. Greenberg, "The President's Initiative to Eliminate Racial and Ethnic Disparities in Health: An Overview," *Journal for Minority Medical Students*, spring 1999, BB3.

29. Sheryl Gay Stolberg, "Black Mothers' Mortality Rate Under Scrutiny," *New York Times*, 8 August 1999, 1.

30. Ronald L. Braithwaite and Sandra E. Taylor, eds., *Health Issues in the Black Community* (San Francisco: Jossey-Bass, 1992), 21.

31. Ellis Cose, *The Rage of a Privileged Class: Why Are Middle-Class Blacks Angry? Why Should America Care?* (New York: HarperCollins, 1993), 39.

32. Ibid., 36.

33. Brigid Schulte, "From the Health Gap: A Special Project," series, with the staff of the Knight-Ridder Washington Bureau; "Research and the Missing Minorities," Knight-Ridder Newspapers series, August 1999.

34. Paul A. Greenberg, "The President's Initiative to Eliminate Racial and Ethnic Disparities in Health: An Overview," *Journal for Minority Medical Students*, spring 1999, BB2.

CHAPTER 4: HOPING AND COPING

1. Aaron T. Beck, A. Weissman, D. Lester, L. Trexler, "The Measurement of Pessimism: The Hopelessness Scale," *Journal of Consulting and Clinical Psychology* 42 (1974): 861–65.

2. Anders Niméus, Lil Träskman-Bendz, and Margot Alsén, "Research Report: Hopelessness and Suicidal Behavior," *Journal of Affective Disorders* 42 (1997): 137–44.

3. Robert H. DuRant et al., "Exposure to Violence and Victimization and Depression, Hopelessness, and Purpose in Life among Adolescents Living in and around Public Housing," *Developmental and Behavioral Pediatrics* 16, no. 4 (1995): 233–37.

4. Jewelle Taylor Gibbs, ed., *Young, Black, and Male in America: An Endangered Species* (Dover, Mass.: Auburn House, 1988).

5. Douglas G. Jacobs, ed., *The Harvard Medical School Guide to Suicide Assessment and Intervention* (San Francisco: Jossey-Bass, 1999), 7.

6. In "The Killer at Thurston High," a special 90-minute edition of PBS's investigative series *Frontline,* the producers revealed portions of a diary written by the teenager Kip Kinkel, who shot and killed his parents and wounded several of his classmates at his Oregon high school. Kinkel wrote extensively about feeling "hopeless" in the weeks before he committed his crimes. The *Frontline* program aired on January 18, 2000, and was produced by Michael Kirk, Karen O'Connor, and Miri Navasky. Additionally, video diaries kept by Dylan Kliebold and Eric Harris were reviewed by *Time* magazine in January 2000, which reported that the two teenage boys, who killed fifteen people including themselves at Columbine High School in Littleton, Colorado, in April of 1999, spoke of their disgust with and anger at the world; in our analysis, a loss of hope, among other psychological issues, clearly influenced their deadly actions.

7. Walter Mosley, *Workin' on the Chain Gang: Shaking Off the Dead Hand of History* (New York: Ballantine, 2000), 10.

8. Stephen Steinberg, *Turning Back: The Retreat from Racial Justice in American Thought and Policy* (Boston: Beacon Press, 1995), 199.

9. U.S. Public Health Service, *The Surgeon General's Call to Action to Prevent Suicide* (Washington, D.C., 1999).

10. Fox Butterfield, *All God's Children: The Bosket Family and the American Tradition of Violence* (New York: Knopf, 1995).

11. Ibid., xv.

12. Ibid.

13. Hussein Abdilahi Bulhan, *Frantz Fanon and the Psychology of Oppression* (Plenum, 1985).

14. U.S. Census figures, 1990.

15. Mari Matsuda, remarks made at the TransAfrica Forum, January 11, 2000, Washington, D.C. (Furthermore, economic reparations alone would be only a small beginning in undoing the centuries of psychological damage caused by racist practices.)

16. Claude Steele and J. Aronson, "Stereotype Threat and the Intellectual Test Performance of African-Americans," *Journal of Personality and Social Psychology* 69 (1995): 797–811; Jeffrey Howard and Ray Hammond, "Rumors of Inferiority: Barriers to Black Success in America," *The New Republic,* 9 September 1985, 17–21.

17. Stephen Steinberg, *Turning Back: The Retreat from Racial Justice in American Thought and Policy* (Boston: Beacon Press, 1995), 199.

18. Cited in Ellis Cose, *The Rage of a Privileged Class: Why Are Middle Class Blacks Angry? Why Should America Care?* (New York: HarperCollins, 1993), 142–43.

19. Ibid., 150.

20. Jan Neeleman, Simon Wessely, and Glyn Lewis, "Suicide Acceptability in African- and White Americans: The Role of Religion," *Journal of Nervous and Mental Disease* 186, no. 1 (1998): 16.

21. Ibid., 12.

22. From the U.S. Centers for Disease Control and Prevention, annual morbidity reports, 1998.

23. Cited in Dorothy Winbush Riley, ed., *My Soul Looks Back, 'Less I Forget* (New York: HarperPerennial, 1995), 195.

24. Ibid., 153.

25. Trevor W. Coleman, "Grown-up Justice," *Emerge*, March 2000, 32–39.

26. Cited in Dorothy Winbush Riley, ed., *My Soul Looks Back, 'Less I Forget* (New York: HarperPerennial, 1995), 195.

CHAPTER 5: "STAY STRONG"

1. Marc Mauer, "Projections for African-American Male Incarceration," in *Intended and Unintended Consequences: State Racial Disparities in Imprisonment* (Washington, D.C.: The Sentencing Project, 1997), 15.

2. Joel Haycock, "Race and Suicide in Jails and Prisons," *Journal of the National Medical Association* 81, no. 4 (1989), 405.

3. Joseph Williams, "Why Are Blacks Less Suicide Prone Than Whites?" *New York Times,* 9 February 1982.

4. John K. Morland, "Racial Recognition by Nursery School Children in Lynchburg, Virginia," *Social Forces* 37 (1958): 132–37.

5. Kevin E. Early, *Religion and Suicide in the African-American Community* (Westport, Conn.: Greenwood, 1992), 42.

6. Ibid., 20.

7. Ibid., 63.

8. Jewelle Taylor Gibbs, "Conceptual, Methodological, and Sociocultural Issues in Black Youth Suicide: Implications for Assessment and Early Intervention," *Suicide and Life-Threatening Behavior* 18, no. 1 (spring 1988): 83.

9. Jewelle Taylor Gibbs, ed., *Young, Black, and Male in America: An Endangered Species* (Dover, Mass.: Auburn House, 1988), 18–19.

10. Ibid., 19.

11. Richard Hoffer, "Feeding Frenzy," *Sports Illustrated*, 7 July 1997, 34–37.

12. Ron Borges, "Tyson Hit with Jail Term in Assault," *Boston Globe*, 6 February 1999, A1.

13. Richard J. Herrnstein and Charles Murray, *The Bell Curve: Intelligence and Class Structure in American Life* (New York: Free Press, 1994).

14. James H. Cone, *The Spirituals and the Blues* (Maryknoll, N.Y.: Orbis Books, 1997), 113.

15. Cited in Kevin E. Early, *Religion and Suicide in the African-American Community* (Westport, Conn.: Greenwood, 1992), 23.

16. Tupac Shakur, "Lord Knows," from *Me Against the World* (New York: Joshuah's Dream/Interscope Pearl Music/Warner-Tamerlane Publishing Corp., BMI, 1995).

CHAPTER 6: BLACKS AND
VICTIM-PRECIPITATED HOMICIDE

1. Alan Feuer, "Drawing a Bead on a Baffling Endgame: Suicide by Cop," *New York Times*, Week in Review section, 21 June 1998.

2. Marvin E. Wolfgang, "Suicide by Means of Victim-Precipitated Homicide," *Journal of Clinical and Experimental Psychopathology and Quarterly Review of Psychiatry and Neurology*, 20 (1959): 335–49.

3. Adam Ramirez, "Racial Tensions Rise after Shooting," *Miami Herald*, 19 July 1999, B1.

4. Adam Ramirez, "Tense Situation: Ft. Lauderdale Police, Community Review Sunday's Sistrunk Shooting," *Miami Herald*, 20 July 1999, B1.

5. Ibid.; author's telephone interview with Carlton Moore, November 1999.

6. Adam Ramirez, "Tense Situation: Ft. Lauderdale Police, Community Review Sunday's Sistrunk Shooting," *Miami Herald*, 20 July 1999, B1.

7. Telephone interview with Carlton Moore, November 1999.

8. Elisabeth Bumiller, "In Wake of Attack, Giuliani Cracks Down on Homeless," *New York Times*, 20 November 1999, A1.

9. Lloyd Gite, "Black Men and Suicide," *Essence*, November 1986, 64.

10. H. Range Hutson, Deirdre Anglin, John Yarbrough, et al., "Suicide by Cop," *Annals of Emergency Medicine* 32, no. 5 (December 1998): 669.

11. Ibid., 667.

12. Ibid.

13. Ibid., 665.

14. Ibid., 668, table 2.

15. Jewelle Taylor Gibbs, "African-American Suicide: A Cultural Paradox," *Suicide and Life-Threatening Behavior* 27, no. 1 (spring 1997): 74.

16. Ibid.

17. Cornel West, lecture on "Race, Nation and Democracy," Harvard Law School, 18 March 1996.

18. In Chicago, white supremacist Benjamin Smith is suspected of killing two people and wounding nine others in a three-day, two-state rampage (William Claiborne, "Child of Privilege Grew into Advocate of Supremacy," *Washington Post*, 6 July 1999, A8); in Los Angeles, Buford Furrow Jr. allegedly enters the North Valley Jewish Community Center and sprays the lobby with automatic gunfire, wounding five people, and later allegedly kills a Filipino postal worker (Evelyn Larrubia, Ted Rohrlich, and Andrew Blankstein, "Community Center Shootings: Suspect Scouted 3 Prominent L. A. Jewish Sites as Targets," *Los Angeles Times*, 13 August 1999, A1).

19. Timothy Egan, "Racist Shootings Test Limits of Health System and Laws," *New York Times*, 14 August 1999, 1.

20. Dr. Poussaint was one of the black psychiatrists who raised the issue of labeling violent racism as a mental health problem with the American Psychiatric Association at its annual meeting in 1969. See Emily Eakin, "Bigotry as Mental Illness or Just Another Norm," *New York Times*, 15 January 2000, A21.

21. U.S. Public Health Service, *The Surgeon General's Call to Action to Prevent Suicide* (Washington, D.C., 1999), 9.

CHAPTER 7: "HE WENT OUT LIKE A MAN"

1. B. A. Botkin, ed., *Lay My Burden Down: A Folk History of Slavery* (Chicago: University of Chicago Press, 1945), 183.

2. U.S. Centers for Disease Control and Prevention, 1998, morbidity & mortality weekly report.

3. Eve K. Moscicki, "Epidemiology of Suicide," in *The Harvard Medical*

School Guide to Suicide Assessment and Intervention, ed. Douglas G. Jacobs (San Francisco: Jossey-Bass, 1999), 41.

4. Jewelle Taylor Gibbs, "Conceptual, Methodological, and Sociocultural Issues in Black Youth Suicide: Implications for Assessment and Early Intervention," *Suicide and Life-Threatening Behavior* 18, no. 1 (spring 1988): 83.

5. Richard Majors and Janet Mancini Billson, *Cool Pose: The Dilemmas of Black Manhood in America* (New York: Lexington Books, 1992).

6. Jewelle Taylor Gibbs, "Conceptual, Methodological, and Sociocultural Issues in Black Youth Suicide: Implications for Assessment and Early Intervention," *Suicide and Life-Threatening Behavior* 18, no. 1 (spring 1988): 81.

7. Michele Wallace, *Black Macho and the Myth of the Superwoman* (New York: Dial Press, 1978), 13.

8. Ntozake Shange, *For Colored Girls Who Have Considered Suicide / When the Rainbow Is Enuf: A Choreopoem* (1976).

9. David Lester, *Suicide in African-Americans* (Commack, N.Y.: Nova Science Publishers, 1998), 69.

10. Julia A. Boyd, *Can I Get a Witness? For Sisters When the Blues Is More Than a Song* (New York: Dutton, 1998), 5–6.

11. Tom Weir, "Direct Leap to NBA Too High for Smith," *USA Today,* 26 November 1999, 1C.

12. Rosemarie Robotham, "Out of the Dark," *Essence,* June 1999, 96.

13. National Medical Association and PeerMed, *Guide to a Healthy Mind for African Americans: A Circle of Hope,* videotape (1999).

CHAPTER 8: THE ROAD AHEAD

1. David Swinton, "Economic Status of African Americans: Limited Ownership and Persistent Inequality," *State of Black America 1992,* ed. Billy J. Tidwell (New York: National Urban League, 1992), 61–117.

2. Otto Kerner, chairman, *Report of the National Advisory Commission on Civil Disorders* (New York: Bantam Book, 1968); Warren Christopher, ed., *Report of the Independent Commission on the Los Angeles Police Department* (Diane Publishing, 1998).

3. Herbert Hendin, *Black Suicide* (New York: Harper Colophon, 1969).

4. Carl C. Bell and Harshad Mehta, "The Misdiagnosis of Black Patients with Manic Depressive Illness," *Journal of the National Medical Association*

72, no. 2 (1980): 141–45; Carl C. Bell and Harshad Mehta, "Misdiagnosis of Black Patients with Manic Depressive Illness: Second in a Series," *Journal of the National Medical Association* 73, no. 2 (1981): 101–107.

5. Alexander Thomas and Samuel Sillen, *Racism and Psychiatry* (New York: Brunner/Mazel, 1972).

6. Richard J. Herrnstein and Charles Murray, *The Bell Curve: Intelligence and Class Structure in American Life* (New York: Free Press, 1994).

7. Charles V. Willie, Bernard M. Kramer, Bertram S. Brown, eds., *Racism and Mental Health* (University of Pittsburgh Press, 1973); Charles V. Willie, Patricia Perri Rieker, Bernard M. Kramer, and Bertram S. Brown, eds., *Mental Health, Racism, and Sexism* (University of Pittsburgh Press, 1995).

8. Alexander Thomas and Samuel Sillen, "The Black Patient: Separate and Unequal," in *Racism and Psychiatry* (New York: Brunner/Mazel, 1972), 135–45.

9. National Medical Association and PeerMed, *Guide to a Healthy Mind for African Americans: A Circle of Hope,* videotape (1999).

10. Daniel Golden, "Casting a Net: Website that Unites Blacks Is Big Ambition of Henry Louis Gates," *Wall Street Journal,* 17 February 2000, 1.

11. Alexander Thomas and Samuel Sillen, "Challenge to the Profession," in *Racism and Psychiatry* (New York: Brunner/Mazel, 1972), 146–57; Charles V. Willie, Patricia Perri Rieker, Bernard M. Kramer, and Bertram S. Brown, eds., *Mental Health, Racism, and Sexism* (University of Pittsburgh Press, 1995).

12. Alexander Thomas and Samuel Sillen, "Challenge to the Profession," in *Racism and Psychiatry* (New York: Brunner/Mazel, 1972), 98.

13. There is a broader area of intelligence not measured by such IQ tests. The theory of multiple intelligences, as formulated by Howard Gardner (*Multiple Intelligences: The Theory in Practice,* Basic Books, New York, 1993), postulates that there are at least seven different intelligences and suggests that commonly used IQ tests only measure two: linguistic intelligence and logical-mathematical intelligence. Other scientists have expanded on these concepts, proposing that there is also an emotional intelligence that comprises an individual's capacity to handle life's challenges and function as a social being (see Daniel Goleman, *Emotional Intelligence,* Bantam Books, New York, 1995).

14. Emily Eakin, "Bigotry as Mental Illness or Just Another Norm," *New York Times,* 15 January 2000, A21.

15. American Psychological Association, "Table 1: Demographic Characteristics of APA Members by Membership Status: 1998," from the 1997 APA directory survey.

16. Wade Nobles, *African Psychology: Toward Its Reclamation, Reascension, and Revitalization* (Oakland, Calif.: Institute for Advanced Study of Black Family Life and Culture, 1986); Joseph L. White, *The Psychology of Blacks: An Afro-American Perspective* (Englewood Cliffs, N.J.: Prentice Hall, 1984).

17. "Learning Cultural Competence," *Journal for Minority Medical Students* 10, no. 1 (1997): BB9.

18. Commonwealth Fund, *National Comparative Survey of Minority Health*, 20 March 1995.

CHAPTER 9: CASTING OFF THE BURDEN

1. U.S. Public Health Service, *The Surgeon General's Call to Action to Prevent Suicide* (Washington, D.C., 1999). Dr. Satcher's comments from a White House press conference announcing the plan, 28 July 1999.

Acknowledgments

First a word of appreciation to Poussaint family members: Christopher W. Poussaint, Lillian MacDowell, Clement Poussaint, Dolores Nethersole, Richard Poussaint, Julia Poussaint, and Bobbie Poussaint; and to Alexander family members: Hazel Fermon, Eric Fermon, Gladys Fermon, Michael Carse, and Anita Carse.

Thanks to the many other individuals who shared with the authors their research, personal insights, technical support, and valuable time. We are particularly grateful for their willingness to be sounding boards as we contemplated the difficult questions surrounding African-American mental health and suicide.

Dr. Sherry Davis Molock, George Washington University; Dr. David Satcher, United States Surgeon General; Dorothy Roberts, Northwestern University School of Law; Dr. Vanessa Northington Gamble, Center for the Study of Race and Ethnicity in Medicine, the University of Wisconsin School of Medicine; Dr. Stephen B. Thomas, Emory University; Dr. Grant Venerable II, Morris Brown College; Dr. David Lester, Richard Stockton College of New Jersey; Dr. Donna Holland Barnes, Southwest Texas University; Vanessa Jackson, M. S. W., director of services and education, Georgia Mental Health Association; Lindsay Hayes, M. S., assistant director, National Center on Institutions and Alternatives.

Steven Gray, staff writer, the *Washington Post;* Tony Pugh, national correspondent, Knight-Ridder Newspapers, Washington, D.C.; Chip Johnson, East Bay columnist, the *San Francisco Chronicle;* Jim Herron Zamora, staff writer, the *San Francisco Examiner;* Bola Cofield, director, Self-Affirming Soul-Healing Africans (SASHA), Berkeley; Mwiza Munthali, TransAfrica Forum, Washington, D.C.; Sgt. Bill Degnan, San Francisco Police Department; Doris Smith, cofounder, National Organization of People of Color Against Suicide, Inc.; Les Franklin, founder and director, the Shaka Franklin Foundation; Pete and Colleen Higgins; and Mike McAlpin.

Tisha Hooks and Helene Atwan at Beacon Press were tremendously supportive and encouraging from the earliest stage of this book's development. The degree of intelligence, commitment, and patience they demonstrated cannot be overstated. We also appreciate the assistance of our agents, Lori Perkins and Ike Williams.

Barbara Sweeny, of the Judge Baker Children's Center, provided exceptional organizational skills, hard work, and attention to detail that made it possible for us to complete *Lay My Burden Down*. Thank you.

And last but not least: thanks to our spouses, Tina Young Poussaint, M.D., and Joseph P. Williams Jr., for their generous patience and support.

Index